First-time
Homeowner's
DIY Manual

Reader's Digest
First-time
Homeowner's
DIY Manual

Expert guidance on DIY tasks for the new homeowner

Published by
The Reader's Digest Association Limited
London • New York • Sydney • Montreal

Contents

Using this book

This is it, you're a homeowner at last – time to set about making your new home your own. From finding a place for your CD collection to finding the stoptap to prevent a flood from a leaking pipe, this book will guide you every step of the way through all the essential DIY tasks: decorating, putting up shelves and dealing with common faults and simple maintenance jobs in your wiring and plumbing.

First things first

Your homebuyer's survey should have alerted you to any major work that needs to be done to your property. But it is also worth taking a little time to get to know your house – how it works and how it is built – so that you can spot problems as soon as they appear and know what to do about them.

Follow the advice in our Home Survey on pages 10–19 to find out what sort of roof you have and what the pitfalls may be, whether you have damp and what might be causing it, and to make sure your home is as secure as it could be.

For even the simplest of DIY tasks, a basic toolkit is a must. Pages 20–25 tell you what you're likely to need, but don't buy everything at once. Build up a well-stocked toolbox gradually by buying a new tool every time you need one for a job. To get you started, make sure you have a hammer, a couple of screwdrivers (flat head and cross-tip), steel tape measure, steel ruler, spirit level, pliers, adjustable spanner and the best power drill you can afford.

Make the place like a home

Once the removal van has turned the corner at the end of the road and the champagne corks have stopped popping, your new home may start to look a little bleak. Boxes everywhere, no curtains at the windows, no pictures on the walls …

Chapter One will help you to make the place feel like home. Before you even start to think about stripping wallpaper or choosing what colour to paint the bedroom, you can make your home more welcoming by putting up the pictures and mirrors you already have. If there are no curtain tracks or poles at the windows it's even more important to get started, so that you can ensure some privacy and shut out the rest of the world at night.

On pages 28–35 you will find everything you need to know about drilling holes safely, driving screws securely or hammering in nails and picture pins for your pictures. You may be hanging flimsy borrowed curtains to see you through until you can buy new, but think ahead and use sturdy fixings that will support better quality, heavier curtains at a later date. Pages 36–39 show you how.

Organise your belongings

When you first move in, it seems as though every room is full of boxes, but there's nowhere to put the contents. With the brilliant storage tips on pages 40–41 you'll soon be on the way to organising your belongings, finding ingenious places to stow everything from clothes to kitchen utensils and cleaning products in the bathroom.

Clear, step-by-step guidance demystifies the baffling process of putting together flat-packed furniture (see pages 42–47), whether it's a simple bathroom cabinet or something more complicated.

Finally, pages 48–53 tell you all you need to know to put up shelves safely and securely – from flexible track shelving

Moving in checklist

☑ **Find your stoptaps** Locate the stoptaps for your water and gas supply (above) and make sure that they turn freely. The gas tap is normally near the meter and the water mains stoptap is usually found in the kitchen.

☑ **Find and read the meters** When you move in, you will need to give meter readings to your gas and electricity providers, and the water supply company, if your house has a water meter.

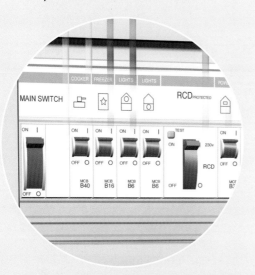

☑ **Find the consumer unit or fuse box** Make sure you know where to switch off the electricity in an emergency. The consumer unit (above) or old-style fusebox should be found next to the electric meter and may be in an understairs cupboard, just inside the front door or in a lockable box on the outside wall of the house.

☑ **Check smoke alarms and carbon monoxide detectors** It is vital that these important safety devices are well-maintained and in good working order. Test the alarms once a month to make sure that the batteries are not flat.

systems to building fixed shelves supported on wooden battens in an alcove next to a chimney breast.

Get creative

Once you've settled in and organised all your worldly goods the fun can start – it's makeover time! Just a simple coat of paint can transform a room, hiding ugly old wallpaper and stamping a bit of your own personality on someone else's old house. But though you may be champing at the bit, don't get carried away too soon. Spend time on preparation at the start and you will have a much better job at the end.

Find out how to prepare the walls, wood and metalwork for painting or papering on pages 56–59, then decide how you're going to decorate them. Pages 60–73 guide you through the task of painting, from choosing and buying the paint, to selecting the right tools and using them professionally. If you plan to hang wallpaper, turn to pages 74–79 for a masterclass on perfecting wrinkle-free walls.

Tiling's not a simple job for beginners, but there's a lot you can do to give a new lease of life to tired old tiles – see pages 80–81 – and we'll show you how to replace a damaged tile with a new one.

And if you're lucky enough to unearth some sound and attractive floorboards when you rip up that old carpet, pages 84–85 show you how you can restore them to their full glory.

When things go wrong

There will inevitably be times when a fuse blows, a tap starts leaking or the toilet won't flush. Don't reach straight for the Yellow Pages and an expensive call-out fee for the professionals. Follow the clear step-by-step advice in Chapters Three and Four and you'll find that you can safely solve many of the most common electrical and plumbing problems, from extending the flex on a table lamp (page 98) to unblocking the kitchen sink (page 113).

Start by getting to know your wiring, plumbing and heating systems and understanding how they work. And make sure you – and everyone else in the house – know how to turn off the water, gas and electricity supplies quickly in the event of an emergency. Pages 88–89 give a quick-reference guide to what to do in an electrical emergency and pages 102–103 do the same for plumbing emergencies, so that even if you cannot safely fix the problem yourself, you can help to minimise the damage while you wait for professional help to arrive.

Remember that there are some jobs, such as anything to do with your gas supply, that must always be done by a professional, and certain regulations with which you must, by law, comply (see right). If you are in any doubt about your ability to complete a job safely, always play it safe and call for help from an expert.

At the back of the book is a list of useful websites and contacts to help you to find reliable tradespeople when you do need to get work done, and a page for you to keep records of when the boiler was last serviced, or to note down contact details for a local emergency locksmith or gas engineer, your insurance details and more.

SAFETY WARNING

Working on your home's electrical and plumbing systems can be dangerous and costly if you make a mistake. Always follow the relevant safety regulations (see right) and only do a job if you feel confident in your ability to do it well. Make sure you know how to switch off the water or electricity immediately if something does go wrong. If you are in any doubt, always call an expert.

Water supply bye-laws

Each water supply company has bye-laws to prevent waste or contamination of the water supply. The bye-laws require you to give your water supplier at least five working days' notice if you intend to install or alter a bidet, a flushing cistern, a tap to which a hose may be connected, or any other fitting which may allow used or stored water to be drawn back into the mains. You can get a copy of the bye-laws from your water supplier.

Gas safety regulations

The Gas Safety (Installation and Use) Regulations make it illegal for anyone who is not 'competent' to carry out work relating to gas supply and fittings. This means leaving all work on your gas supply and equipment to a qualified gas fitter, registered with CORGI (The Council for Registered Gas Installers).

Wiring regulations

Since January 2005, all new domestic wiring work in England and Wales must comply with the requirements of a new section of the Building Regulations. Part P, entitled Electrical Safety, covers the design, installation, inspection and testing of electrical work in the home. It applies to both DIY and professional electrical work. See page 92 for more information about what you can and cannot do yourself.

GET TO KNOW YOUR CENTRAL HEATING

Efficient temperature and time controls can save a great deal of money on fuel bills.

Room thermostat

This temperature-sensitive switch is set to a pre-selected room temperature. It sends an electrical signal to switch the heating on when the air temperature falls below the pre-set level, and off when it rises above the level.

Thermostatic radiator valve

The best means of controlling the temperature in each room is to fit a thermostatic radiator valve (TRV) to each radiator. The valve opens and closes according to the temperature in the room. If the room is cold, a full flow is allowed through to the radiator. Then as the room warms up, the valve closes to reduce the hot water flow through the radiator.

Rooms facing south and rooms with open fires or other heat producing appliances, such as an oven, benefit most from TRVs.

Most systems are suitable for use with thermostatic radiator valves. Seek expert advice on which ones to buy.

TRVs do not control the central heating pump and boiler, so they must be combined with a room thermostat and programmer.

Programmers

Time controls range from simple switches to complex electronic programmers.

The most useful can time space heating and domestic hot water separately, so water heating can be turned on and off at the same times of day all year round, while space heating times can vary with the season.

Electronic types can give you three control periods a day and different settings for every day of the week. Some even have a 'holiday' setting.

Water heating control

The hot water temperature is often controlled only by the boiler thermostat. So hot water to the taps is at the same temperature as the water supplied to the radiators. This is probably hotter than necessary.

An electric thermostat fitted on the outside of the hot water cylinder will restrict the temperature of the water inside. It switches a motorised valve on and off to control the flow of water passing through the heating coil inside the cylinder.

Boiler energy management

Sophisticated devices make sure that the boiler works only when needed.

A boiler energy manager will reduce wasteful short cycling on a boiler – that is, when 'hot water only' is selected on a conventional central heating programmer, the boiler will continually switch on and off to keep the water in the boiler at the selected temperature. It will do this even though the hot water cylinder is already full of hot water. This 'short cycling' can add as much as 30 per cent to fuel bills.

The boiler energy manager will also take account of outside temperatures, and will regulate the central heating system accordingly. For example it will override the setting and delay the start time of the central heating on warmer days.

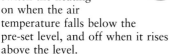

How your home was built

The age of your home will dictate how it was built. The construction of houses built in the last fifty years or so differs markedly from those put up before about 1920. Houses built during the intervening generation of change incorporate both traditional house-building techniques and some of the new methods of construction that were being introduced.

Knowing how your home is built before hiring professionals – or tackling any DIY task – could save you time and money. Understanding how the roof, walls and floors are put together and what they're made of will help you to plan improvements and alterations, and deal with any faults that might develop as time goes by.

The roof

Old roofs are usually covered with natural slates or clay tiles, and were designed to take the weight of these. If you are considering having them replaced with concrete tiles, bear in mind that these are usually much heavier, meaning that the roof timbers will need to be strengthened, too. If the timbers do need reinforcing, the cost is likely to cancel out any saving you might make by re-roofing with manufactured tiles – in which case, you're better off leaving the roof structure alone and replacing like with like.

How is your roof constructed?
A glance in the loft will tell you what sort of roof you have. Traditional timber roofs, assembled on site, have open space below the rafters for storage. Roofs constructed in the past 50 years usually have roof trusses – prefabricated timber frames incorporating rafters and ceiling joists. These are factory-made so the roof structure can be erected quickly, but the design and number of the trusses leaves little room for storage.

Save boarding on a roof
If you live in an older house with a boarded roof – one with planking laid across the tops of the rafters – don't have it stripped off if you ever have a new roof put on the property. The boarding insulates the roof space far better than a layer of roofing felt alone, and areas which are rotten can be replaced easily with sections of new pressure-treated wood.

Suspended and solid ground floors

Ground floors in houses built before about 1950 are usually covered with floorboards laid over timber joists which are suspended over an underfloor airspace. Over the past 50 or so years, solid concrete ground floors have become the norm, although they may be overlaid with timber strip flooring or chipboard.

Accessing and altering plumbing and heating pipework under a timber floor is a relatively simple matter; getting at pipes buried in concrete is much more difficult.

Problems with concrete floors
Concrete floors in the kitchens and sculleries of old houses are prone to rising damp because they were laid straight onto the earth, with no separating damp-proof membrane (DPM). Inherent dampness in a solid floor also makes it cold and liable to condensation. Where concrete floors have been laid next to wooden ones, they can hinder ventilation of the underfloor space, increasing the risk of rot in the wood floor. Building Regulations now ensure that concrete ground floors are underlaid with a DPM of heavy-grade polythene. Since 1990 they have also had to be insulated.

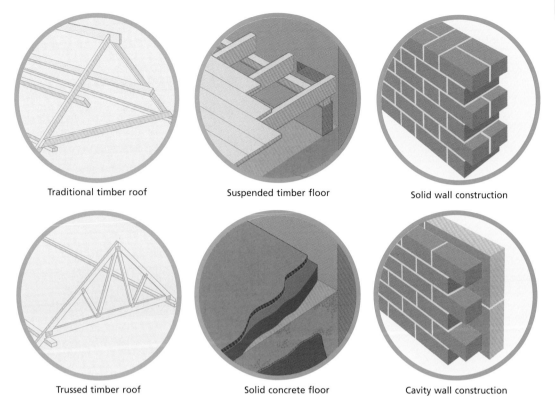

Traditional timber roof

Suspended timber floor

Solid wall construction

Trussed timber roof

Solid concrete floor

Cavity wall construction

Problems with wooden floors

In older homes, the ends of the joists supporting timber ground floors are embedded in external walls, making them prone to rot if the walls are damp. The square-edge floorboards used until the 1930s let in underfloor draughts – a problem largely cured by the use of tongue-and-groove boards, although at the cost of making the boards harder to lift.

Two kinds of external brick walls

Solid all the way through

The bricks in solid walls are laid in patterns known as bonds. What all solid walls have in common are headers – bricks laid end-on so that they pass right through the wall to give it strength. A solid wall will be as thick as the length of a brick (215mm) plus the thickness of plaster inside and any rendering outside. You can measure the wall at a door or window opening.

A cavity in the middle

Only the long faces of bricks, known as stretchers, are on view if your house has cavity walls. The walls are a minimum of 255mm thick (two single leaves of brickwork, each 102.5mm thick, separated by a 50mm wide cavity), and more if the cavity is wider or the internal leaf is built of thicker blockwork.

Cavity walls have several advantages over solid ones. Any rain that penetrates the outer leaf of brickwork cannot bridge the cavity and instead runs down its inner face to ground level, so the inner leaf stays dry. Interior wall surfaces are warmer because the air in the cavity acts as an insulator, and extra insulation placed in the cavity during or after building makes them warmer still.

Timber-framed houses have an inner leaf consisting of load-bearing wooden wall panels clad with external plywood sheathing and filled with insulation.

Assessing the condition of your property

Carry out a survey to make sure your home is weathertight, safe and thief-proof before you do anything else. There's no point in decorating if the roof is letting in rain, or installing new light fittings if the wiring is dangerous and needs replacing. And if the house isn't secure, filling it with expensive fixtures and fittings before making sure that all the exterior doors and windows have good locks is also getting your priorities wrong.

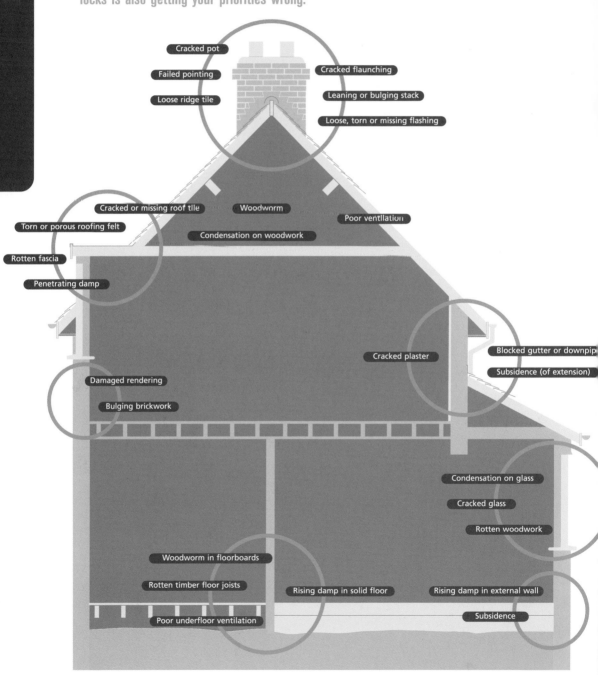

Cracked pot

Failed pointing

Loose ridge tile

Cracked flaunching

Leaning or bulging stack

Loose, torn or missing flashing

Cracked or missing roof tile

Woodworm

Poor ventilation

Torn or porous roofing felt

Condensation on woodwork

Rotten fascia

Penetrating damp

Cracked plaster

Blocked gutter or downpipe

Subsidence (of extension)

Damaged rendering

Bulging brickwork

Condensation on glass

Cracked glass

Rotten woodwork

Woodworm in floorboards

Rotten timber floor joists

Rising damp in solid floor

Rising damp in external wall

Poor underfloor ventilation

Subsidence

Take it from the top

Start your home survey with the roof. A pair of binoculars is useful for inspecting it without having to climb a ladder. If you can't see the whole roof surface from your garden or the street, ask to view it from a neighbour's property.

Check the controls

Before you start any DIY, make sure you know where the water and gas stoptaps and main electricity supply switch are located. Keep a torch by the electricity meter, plus some fuse wire (see page 23) if the system has fuses. Locate all drain inspection chambers (manholes) and check that the covers can be lifted easily if a drain becomes blocked.

Inspect the loft

Go into the loft to inspect the underside of the roof. Look for water stains on the timbers, or wait until there's a heavy downpour and then look for signs of rain getting in. There should be ventilators along the eaves, at the ridge, in gable walls or on the roof slope. Shine a light along the eaves if there are none to be seen, because a badly ventilated roof space can be liable to dry rot, and this often sets in along the eaves. Lastly, examine the roof timbers for evidence of woodworm.

Stacks of trouble

Chimneys are the most exposed part of your house, so check them closely for signs of damage. Look for cracks in the pots and in the flaunching – the mortar bed in which the pots are embedded.

If a stack is built against an outside wall, examine it for straightness. The combination of coal gases condensing inside the flue and rain soaking through the mortar joints can set up a chemical reaction which makes the brickwork bulge outwards. Repointing the brickwork and lining the flue can arrest the problem, but a severely damaged stack may have to be completely rebuilt.

Include the garden

Remember to survey the garden at the same time as the rest of your home. Fences may be in poor condition, a shed roof may be leaking, garden paths may need lighting, and nearby trees may be undermining boundary walls. A gate or door into the garden might need a lock fitting to it.

Look for overflows

Check the gutters and downpipes for blockages. Stains on the house walls can reveal where previous overflows have occurred. The next time it rains, check where gutters are overflowing or where water is leaking from downpipe joints.

Is the woodwork sound?

Prod the external woodwork with a bradawl to detect rot under the paintwork, and look round the edges of door and window frames for gaps where rainwater can penetrate – especially on north and west-facing walls, which are the most exposed to the weather.

That sinking feeling

Subsidence is the most serious problem you might detect. It occurs most commonly on clay soil, which expands when wet and then contracts as it dries out. Look at the corners of your house and at the door and window openings. Are they vertical and square?

Zigzag cracks running down the walls from the corners of door and window frames, and between the main house and an extension, are signs of possible subsidence. Inside, doors and windows may start jamming for no apparent reason, and wallpaper can crease or tear.

Barriers to rising damp

Look for a damp-proof course (DPC) – visible outside between the second and third courses of brickwork above ground level. This is a horizontal band of slate, bituminous felt or black polythene. In an older house built before DPCs were introduced, you may see a row of small mortar or rubber plugs indicating that a chemical DPC has been injected into the walls in recent years.

Where the air gets in

Airbricks or grilles are built into the outside walls, just above ground level, in houses with suspended timber ground floors. These allow air to circulate in the underfloor space, helping to keep it dry and to discourage rot. Make sure they are not blocked or obstructed in any way.

Testing timber floors

Jump up and down on timber ground floors. If they move noticeably, the joists may be rotten because their ends are built into walls suffering from rising damp. Prod skirting boards with a bradawl to see if they're rotten – another indication that there may be problems beneath the floor.

Diagnosing damp and tracing the causes

Damp problems in a house can be due to a number of causes – rain getting through the walls or roof, moisture being absorbed from the ground, condensation settling on cold surfaces, or a mixture of these. Make sure you know what the cause of dampness is before trying to cure it, otherwise you may be dealing only with part of the problem, or even adopting the wrong remedy for the sort of damp involved.

Spot the tell-tale semicircles

In an old house with a slate damp-proof course (DPC), slight movement of the building can crack the slates, allowing damp from the ground to rise into the masonry above the crack. A single point failure will cause a semicircular patch of damp up to 1m or so across, while multiple cracks will lead to an almost continuous band across the affected wall.

Try the foil test

If you're not sure of the cause of a damp patch on a wall, try the foil test. Dry the wall surface with a fan heater, then tape some kitchen foil tightly over the damp area. If the surface of the foil is wet after 24 hours, you have condensation. If the foil is dry but the wall surface beneath it is damp, you have rising or penetrating damp. Discount rising damp if the moisture is more than 1m above outside ground level.

Getting through the gaps

Patches of dampness on walls around windows and doors are usually caused by rain getting through gaps between their frames and the surrounding masonry. Where the damp is below the opening, it may be because there is no drip groove to stop the water creeping under a projecting sill or threshold. If there is a drip groove, make sure the rain is not crossing it because it is blocked with paint or mortar.

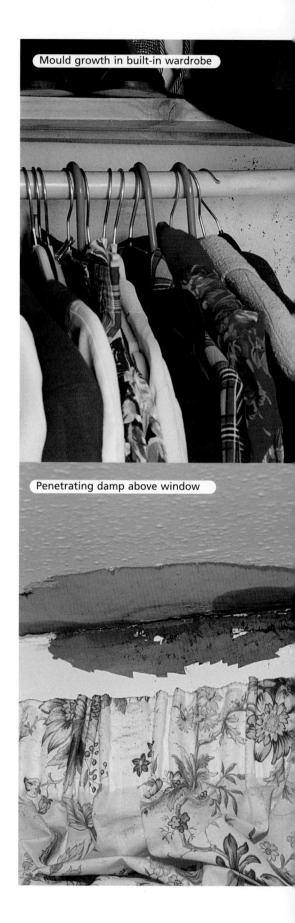

Mould growth in built-in wardrobe

Penetrating damp above window

Checking the loft space

Looking for a leak in the roof

Discovering exactly where a pitched roof is leaking can be difficult. Rain can trickle down the roofing felt and then along the sides of rafters before it drips onto the loft floor. Look for clues such as dampness on a party wall or chimney stack in the loft, which might indicate that flashings are defective or missing. Getting someone to spray a hose on the roof, area by area, while you remain inside the loft can also help to reveal where the water is getting in.

Woodworm at work

At the same time as checking lofts, underfloor spaces and built-in cupboards for signs of dampness, inspect structural timbers and joinery for evidence of woodworm, which thrives in slightly damp environments. Look for the small flight holes made by the beetles when they emerge from the wood and the fine wood dust created by the pest. Check the untreated backs of all freestanding chests and wardrobes, and the unpainted top and bottom edges of doors at the same time.

Suspect condensation

If the roof isn't leaking but the timbers and loft insulation are damp, the likely culprit is condensation. This is caused by warm moisture-laden air rising into the loft from the rooms below and condensing on cold surfaces within the loft space. In serious cases, roof timbers can rot and saturated insulation materials can stain ceilings.

Check out the plumbing

Leaks in plumbing and central-heating pipework can cause damp patches which could be misinterpreted as rising or penetrating damp. This is especially common where the pipes are run beneath a floor or are buried in wall plaster. Here a pinhole leak or a weeping fitting can release surprisingly large volumes of water as time goes by, especially if it has no chance to dry out naturally.

If this is the cause of the problem, you have two possible courses of action. You can either expose the fault and then replace the affected pipes, which will cause a lot of disruption. Alternatively, you can simply leave them where they are and bypass them by installing new ones.

Prod the paintwork

Use a bradawl to test the soundness of skirting boards if there are signs of damp in downstairs walls or the underfloor space. The backs of skirting boards are usually left unpainted, so they readily absorb moisture from the masonry. However, severe deterioration of the boards is often not apparent because of paint applied to their face sides.

Check the damp-proof course

If you think you have rising damp in your house, locate the damp-proof course (DPC) and make sure it isn't covered by a flower bed, path, drive or patio. Look for rendering that has been applied over the DPC. Check whether there is a vertical DPC sandwiched between the house wall and the end of a garden wall built up against it. Curing these common causes of rising damp will solve the problem for little or no cost, saving you from incurring an expensive bill from a professional damp-proofing firm.

Is a guarantee required?

Installing a DPC in an older house usually involves drilling holes into the second or third course of brickwork above outdoor ground level, then pumping a chemical waterproofer into the walls. You can hire the equipment and do the job yourself if you don't need the guarantee.

Allow time for drying out

If your home needs a DPC, schedule it into the order of work as early as possible. The plaster on damp walls will have absorbed salts from the masonry and will have to be hacked off to a height of about 1m before the DPC is installed. Then the masonry will need to be left bare for several months so that it can dry out before the walls are replastered – either with a traditional sand and cement plaster, or with one recommended by the damp-proofing company.

Combat condensation

Let your house breathe

Open windows when the weather is fine so that drier air can get in. Fit extractor fans with humidity detectors in kitchens and bathrooms to remove moist air automatically, or else plug in a dehumidifier. Lastly, remember that sealing up doors, windows and unused flues to eliminate draughts will increase the likelihood of condensation.

Try small adjustments first

You can hold condensation at bay by spending more on keeping the house warm – turning up the central heating and improving the insulation. Often, however, marginal adjustments – slightly more ventilation combined with a low but constant level of background heat – are just as effective, and cheaper.

Easy ways to cut humidity

Create less moisture by drying clothes outdoors whenever possible. If you have a tumble drier, vent it to the outside.

Condensation on single glazing

Keep lids on boiling saucepans and shut bathroom and kitchen doors to stop steam spreading through the house.

Use dehumidifiers in damp, enclosed areas and avoid heaters that run on paraffin or oil – both fuels produce large quantities of water vapour when burned.

Made to absorb moisture
Decorate kitchens and bathrooms with paint specially made for these rooms. Ordinary emulsion will flake or develop mould if it gets damp frequently, but anti-condensation paint is designed to absorb moisture from damp air and release it back into the atmosphere when the air is drier.

Damp-proof plaster
If condensation is severe, on north-facing walls for example, have them replastered with an anti-condensation plaster. Like kitchen and bathroom paint, this product absorbs moisture when the atmosphere is damp and releases it when it is dry. The plaster also contains small air bubbles which insulate the surface, helping to further reduce the risk of condensation.

Upgrading locks on external doors

A mortise deadlock is commonly used as a second lock on a front door that already has a cylinder lock. It is recessed into a slot cut in the edge of the door, and shoots a bolt into a hole in the door frame. The more levers the lock has, the harder it is to pick.

Pick five levers
Look at the faceplate of the mortise lock fitted on your front door. If the information stamped on it says it has less than five levers, upgrade it straightaway to make it more burglar-proof. Most insurance companies now require five-lever locks at least. One with seven levers is better still.

Avoid the joint
Fit a mortise lock about a third of the way up a door, below the middle rail or horizontal, if possible. Otherwise, you will have to cut into the joint securing the rail and stile (upright) together.

Better safe than sorry

Who's there? A door viewer, or peephole, is a valuable security device, but is of little use after darkness unless your doorstep is well lit. Keep the porch light switched on after dusk, or fit a sensor-activated light that will come on whenever someone approaches the door.

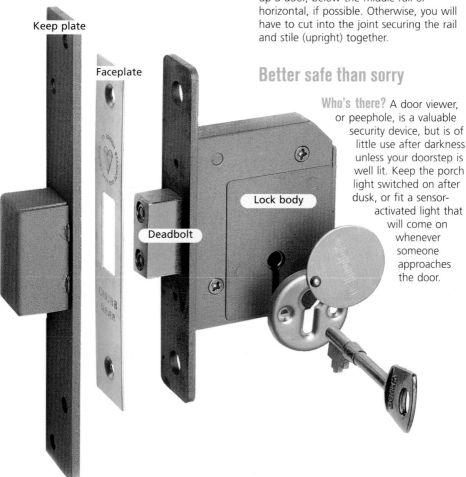

Keep plate

Faceplate

Lock body

Deadbolt

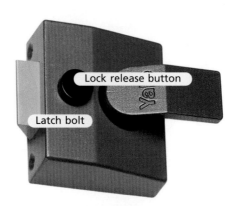

Staple

Lock release button

Latch bolt

Dead secure

Fit a deadlocking cylinder nightlatch (above) instead of a standard type if your front door is glazed. When locked from outside, the indoor handle cannot be operated, so a burglar cannot get in by breaking the glass, reaching through and turning it as he can with a non-deadlocking type.

Check the wood

A lock is only as strong as the door and frame in which it is fitted. Replace fragile wood before fitting new locks. Also, one lock may not be enough to secure against determined force. Fit the cylinder and mortise locks at different heights so as to spread the load of any blows to the door. Buy only locks that conform to British Standard BS 3621.

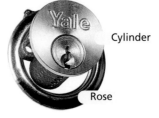

Cylinder

Rose

Reinforcement for a cylinder latch

One way to give your front door extra security at relatively low cost and with very little DIY work is to fit reinforcements to the door, the frame, or both.

Make the front door more resistant to forcing

The strongest chain

The strongest door chains have a right-angled plate which fixes into the side of the rebate and turns round the frame edge. These are highly resistant to forcing. You can strengthen an existing fitting by exchanging the screws supplied with the chain for longer ones.

Doors secured with a rim lock or cylinder latch are quite easily forced: a heavy blow drives the latch against the staple, which is held in place by just a couple of screws, shearing it away from the inside face of the frame and allowing an intruder to get in. A reinforcement bar, sometimes known as a London bar (above) is designed to prevent this happening. It consists of a long steel bar shaped to fit tightly over the staple and is fixed all the way down the inside face of the frame with screws.

Improving window and door security

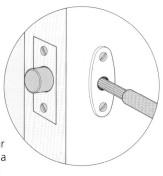

Fit concealed bolts

Fit rack bolts in pairs to external doors and to casement windows – one near the top corner and the other near the bottom. The bolt engages in a hole in the frame. They are more secure than surface-mounted locks, and are also much less obtrusive.

Block the handles

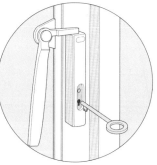

Screw a cockspur bolt to a metal-framed window to stop an intruder operating the handle after breaking the glass. The key locks the bolt in the up position, and lets it drop when you want to open the window. Avoid cracking the glass by drilling no deeper than necessary when making holes for the bolt's self-tapping screws.

Push-button locks

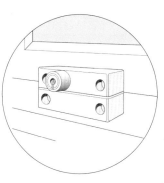

Make sure wooden windows are always secure by fitting locks that don't need a key to lock them. With some types, you simply push a button in to secure the two parts of the lock together after closing the window. Other types lock together automatically as the parts meet. Both need a key to undo them.

Lock the window stay

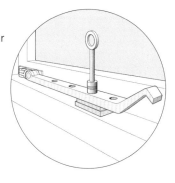

If you want security plus the option of leaving a window ajar for ventilation, and the window has a stay pierced with holes, replace the plain peg on which the stay normally fits with a casement stay lock. You can then secure the window in any position by attaching the screw-on lock to the threaded peg with the key, which is also used to unlock it.

Bolt sliding sashes together

Fit dual screws – one at each side of the meeting rails – to secure sash windows. These consist of an internally threaded barrel that passes through the inner rail, and a bolt that passes through the barrel and screws into the outer rail.

Emergency cover

A cracked or broken window leaves your home vulnerable to intruders, as well as letting in draughts and rain.

Seal a cracked pane temporarily with transparent waterproof glazing tape, applied to the outside. If the pane is smashed, cover the whole window with heavy-gauge polythene secured by timber battens nailed round the frame. If good security is vital, nail a sheet of plywood across the window frame until you can replace the glass.

Tape a cracked pane

If glass is cracked but intact, crisscross the pane with masking tape to lessen the risk of flying shards when you break it, then use a hacking knife to remove the putty. Break the pane from inside with a hammer and a block of wood. Lift out large shards first, then chip out and remove the smaller pieces.

Basic toolkit

The following pages describe the tools you will
need to tackle all the run-of-the-mill DIY jobs you
are likely to face as a new householder. These
include tasks as diverse as changing a plug,
bleeding a radiator, filling a crack in the
plaster or hanging a picture.

Top layer for
quick access

Second layer for
cutting tools

Bottom layer for
oils, solvents and
other liquids

Drawers for
nails and screws

Organising your toolkit Most modern tool boxes have multiple stacking layers.
Avoid metal tool boxes; they are heavy to carry around and they rust. Put tools to
which you need quick access in the top layer. Store cutting tools, such as chisels
or knives, in the second layer where they are safely out of the way but not loose
in the base of the toolbox. Keep liquids in the bottom layer, in case they leak.

Screwdrivers

Within reason, you can never have too many screwdrivers. Screws come with head recesses of different types, ranging from straight slots to cross and hexagon shapes, and in different sizes.

To start with, you need a flat-tip screwdriver with a blade about 125mm long for slotted-head screws, and a No. 2 Phillips cross-tip screwdriver which will also drive other types of cross-head screws such as Pozidriv and Prodrive.

You will also need a small electrician's screwdriver for fiddly jobs. This has an insulated handle, for safety's sake.

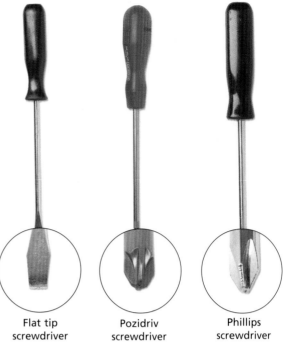

Electrician's
screwdriver

Hexagon keys

Flat tip
screwdriver

Pozidriv
screwdriver

Phillips
screwdriver

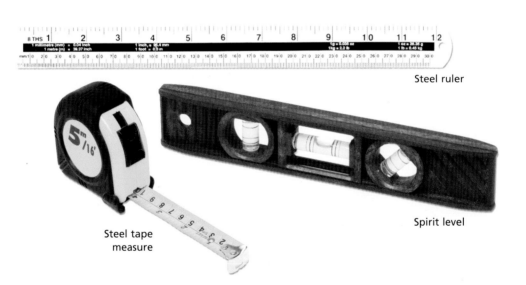

Steel ruler

Steel tape
measure

Spirit level

Measuring tools

A steel or aluminium straightedge is essential for many DIY jobs, from checking the flatness of surfaces (a tiled wall, for example) to guiding a trimming knife.

You need a steel tape measure for measuring and estimating jobs. An ideal size is a 5m tape, which will cope with measuring up a room as well as taking smaller measurements. Most have metric and imperial markings, so you can use the tape as a handy conversion device. Pick one with a lock that keeps the blade extended while you use it.

You will need a spirit level if you are to get things like shelves and curtain tracks level. It is a plastic or alloy bar with vials containing an air bubble set into the long edge and usually at each end. The level is horizontal or vertical when the bubble is exactly centred between the marks on the appropriate vial.

Pincers   Pliers

Pincers and pliers

Pincers are extremely useful jacks of all trades. They are designed primarily for pulling out unwanted pins, tacks and nails – from floorboards, for example – but can also be used for pulling out picture hooks without damaging the plaster, or nibbling awkward shapes out of ceramic tiles. Pincers are usually about 200mm long, and are inexpensive to buy.

A pair of combination pliers is well worth having in your tool kit. Their serrated jaws are useful for gripping all sorts of things, such as the wire loop that holds the bath plug on its chain or the shattered remains of a light bulb stuck in its lampholder. You can also twist and cut wire with them, and straighten bent metal – and even use them as a makeshift spanner if none is to hand.

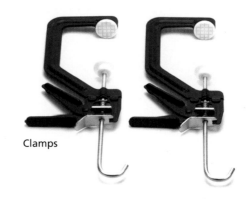

Getting a grip

Clamps are not a vital component of the first time homeowner's toolkit, but are very useful for holding items securely on the workbench, for example when cutting curtain track to length. They are also used to clamp woodworking joints together while the adhesive sets.

Clamps

Radiator key

This is an essential tool for bleeding air from the central heating system (see page 122). If a radiator is cool at the top and warm at the bottom, then air is probably trapped at the top and needs to be released.

Radiator key

Adjustable spanner

Adjustable spanner

Spanners are better at turning nuts and bolts than pliers. What you need is an adjustable spanner with a jaw opening up to about 30mm.

Sink plunger

This is the tool to use when the kitchen sink outlet is blocked with solidified fat or other debris (see page 113).

Plunger

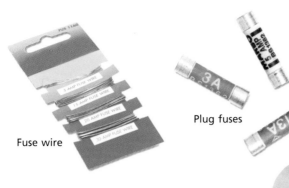

Fuse wire

Plug fuses

Fuses and fuse wire
Plug fuses occasionally blow and should always be replaced with one of the same rating. You will need fuse wire only if your house has an old-style fuse box.

Wire cutters and strippers
Wire cutters simply cut cable to length; wire strippers will remove the plastic insulation from around the cores – very useful when fitting a plug.

Cable and pipe detector
Use a cable detector as a precaution to check for hidden pipes or cables before driving nails or drilling holes for wall fixings.

Torch

Torch
A battery-powered torch is invaluable in a power cut. Check batteries regularly and keep a set of spares in the toolbox.

Wire stripper

Wire cutters

Cable detector

Light machine oil or 'three-in-one'

Aerosol water repellent (WD40)

White spirit

Wet and dry abrasive paper

Clean, smooth and lubricate
Abrasive paper is needed for finishing new wood, keying the surface of paintwork before redecorating it, and removing surplus material such as plaster filler. White spirit is needed for thinning and removing wet oil-based paint; oils are used for lubrication and repelling water.

Hammers

Every toolbox needs a claw hammer, which will drive all but the smallest pins and can also be used to lever out old nails by fitting the grooved claw under the nail head.

To accompany your claw hammer, buy a nail punch. This small steel tool is used with a hammer to drive nail heads below the surface of the wood they are fixing.

A small pin hammer or lightweight ball-pein hammer is used for driving small nails and panel pins.

Knife

A trimming knife is a DIY essential. A standard blade will cut paper and card and thin sheet materials such as plasterboard, and will mark clear cutting lines on all sorts of surfaces. One with a retractable blade is safer to use and to carry around. Most knives allow you to store spare blades inside the handle.

Filling knife

This tool has a flexible steel blade, and is used for applying filler to holes and cracks in wood or plaster.

Junior hacksaw

Junior hacksaws take slim, 150mm replaceable blades, and are used to cut through metal, such as a rusty nail or bolt or an unwanted pipe, or plastic – curtain track, for example. They can also be used for cutting slim timber mouldings.

Tenon saws

If you plan to cut any wood larger than a slim moulding, you need a proper saw. A tenon saw has a rectangular blade about 250mm long stiffened along the top with a strip of brass or steel. It will cope with all sorts of minor woodwork jobs such as trimming wall battens or cutting a shelf to length. The thickness of wood it will cut is limited by the depth of the blade.

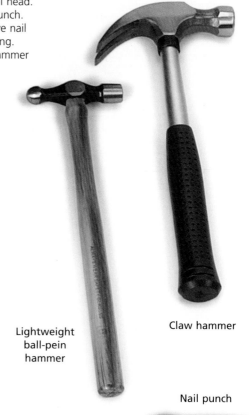

Claw hammer

Lightweight
ball-pein
hammer

Nail punch

Trimming knife

Tenon saw

Filling knife

Junior hacksaw

22 16 13

Screwdriver
drill bits

Flat wood
drill bits

Cordless
drill

14.4V

Countersink
drill bit

Twist
drill bits

Masonry
drill bits

Power drill
You will need a power drill for all sorts of DIY jobs.
The most versatile is a cordless drill, which has a
rechargeable battery and can be used anywhere
without the need for a power supply. However,
cordless models are not as powerful as mains-
powered drills, and can be more expensive. Choose
a drill rated at 14.4 or 18V.
   You will also need a range of drill bits. Twist drill
bits make holes in wood and metal; masonry bits
make holes in solid walls, usually to take wallplugs
when making wall fixings; flat wood bits drill larger
holes in wood and boards, and come in sizes from
12mm up to 32mm; and a countersink drill bit is
used to make cone-shaped recesses to accept the
heads of countersunk screws.
   Screwdriver bits enable you to use a cordless
drill (set to a slow speed) as a power screwdriver.

Stepladder

Access and work
A light but sturdy stepladder is vital for
high-level work. Make sure the feet
have non-skid covers. Accessories such
as paint hooks are useful.
   The last essential for everyday DIY is
a portable workbench. You can use it
to support things while you cut, drill
and assemble them, and its jaws will
act as a large vice for gripping anything
from a length of pipe to a room door.
You can even stand on it at a pinch.
Small basic types are surprisingly cheap.

Portable
workbench

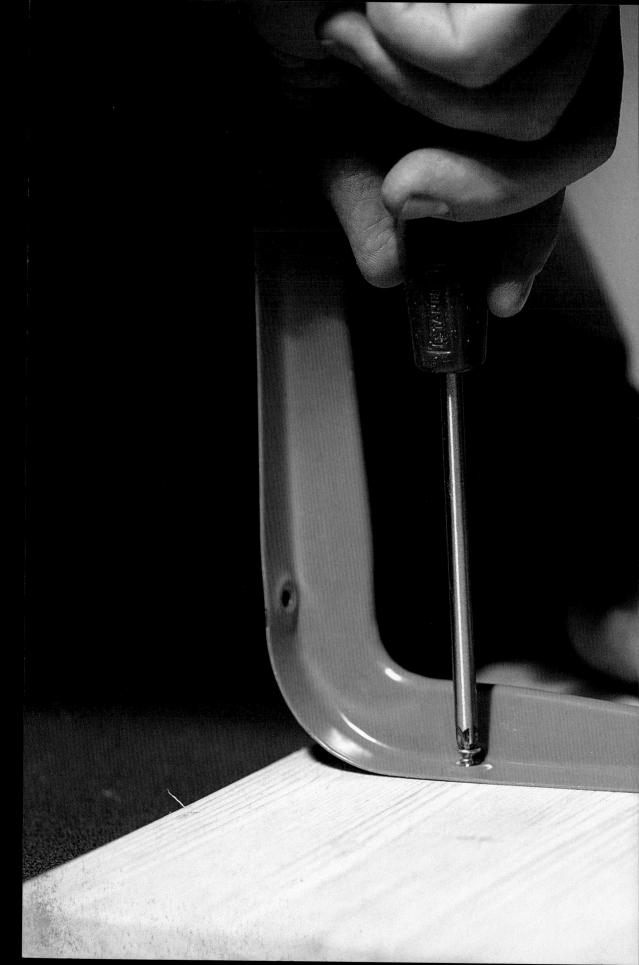

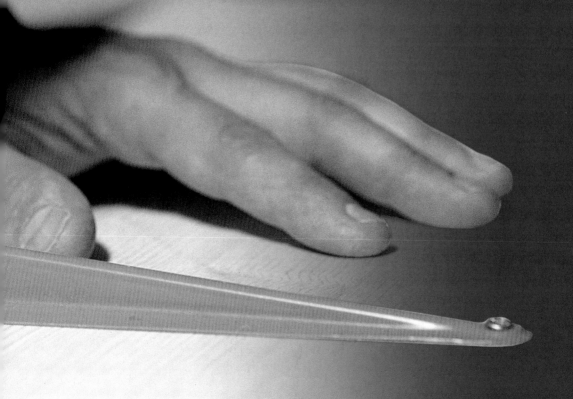

Making a
home your
own

Drilling holes

There are few DIY jobs that do not involve drilling a hole at some stage. You will need your cordless or mains-powered drill for all these operations, along with a range of drill bits.

Locating concealed hazards

A cable and pipe detector is a hand-held battery-powered electronic device that will reveal the presence of electricity cables or plumbing pipework concealed in the house structure. It is important to be aware of their presence whenever you are making fixings (with nails or with screws and wallplugs) into a wall, floor or ceiling, since piercing one could cause personal injury, physical damage or both.

In some cases it is obvious where buried services are located. For example, you can expect there to be a vertical cable run immediately above a light switch, or pipework above or below a flush-mounted thermostatic shower mixer valve. In other cases, using the detector can avoid a potential accident.

Some detectors will locate only live electrical cables; others will detect any buried metal – cable, pipework, even the line of nails fixing plasterboard to a hidden wall stud or ceiling joist.

Switch the detector on and set its sensitivity according to the manufacturer's instructions. Pass it slowly back and forth over the area you are testing. The detector will bleep and may flash a light when it senses a hazard, enabling you to mark and avoid its route when making any fixings.

Get to know your drill

Cordless drills run on rechargeable batteries, and most come with two batteries. Make sure you know how to remove and insert the batteries, and how to operate the battery charger. Check whether the battery can be left to trickle-charge for hours, or whether it has a fixed recharge time.

Next, read the instructions. These will tell you how to select the following:
• forward and reverse gears
• the correct speed setting for drilling, screwdriving and, if the drill has the option, hammer action for making holes in masonry
• the correct torque setting, which enables you to apply the optimum turning force when driving screws into different materials.

Most cordless drills come with a carry case. Keep the drill in it when you are not using it. If you do not have a case, buy one. DIY stores stock a selection; take your drill in to test its fit before you buy.

Fitting drill bits

Select the right type of drill bit for the job you are doing (see page 25).

1 Open the chuck by twisting the knurled ring and fit the end of the drill bit inside it.

2 Tighten the locking ring until you feel it start to slip. The drill bit is now secure. Select forward gear and the drilling or hammer-drilling option, and you are ready to start work.

Drilling freehand

Most people drill holes by simply pointing the drill at the surface and squeezing the trigger. With very few exceptions, drilled holes have to be at 90° to the surface.

1 If you have a good eye, check from two angles that you are holding the drill at more or less the right angle. This is good enough for many drilling jobs.

2 If you want to check the angle more accurately, hold the drill in position and set a try square against the surface you are drilling into. The drill bit should be parallel with the metal blade of the try square.

Drilling holes in tiles

Stop drill bits from skating

Make fixings in tiled walls by drilling into the grout lines wherever possible. If you have to drill through the face of the tile, use a sharp spear-point or masonry drill bit so the glaze doesn't chip. Stop the bit from skating on the glaze by sticking masking tape on the tile where you want to drill; this will give the bit an initial 'bite'.

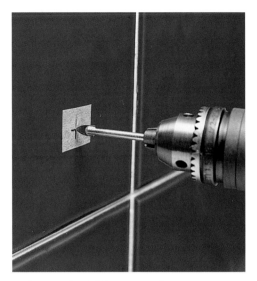

Make sure the drill isn't set on hammer action and start slowly if it has variable speed control.

Sink the plug

If you're inserting a wall plug into a tiled wall, drill the hole at least 3mm deeper than the length of the plug so it can be pushed into the wall past the tile. Otherwise, when a screw is driven into the plug, the sideways pressure it exerts may crack the tile.

Sealed against moisture

Apply waterproof silicone sealant to the tips of screws when mounting fixtures on tiled walls that get wet. As the screw tightens in the wall plug, the sealant is forced up the threads, helping to stop water getting down the fixing and behind the tiles.

Picking the right screws and plugs for wall fixings

Cross-head screws are easier to drive than slotted head types, especially if you are using your cordless drill as a power screwdriver. Make sure that the wall plug is the right size for the screw you are using, and that the screw is large enough to do the job you want it to. There's no point in putting up a track for heavy curtains with short, skinny screws – it will inevitably fall down. And using a weak fixing to hold up a shelf could be dangerous.

Gripping in plasterboard

If you want to fix something fairly light in weight directly to plasterboard, you can use a plug that's screwed into a pilot hole. The plug has a coarse thread which bites into the core of the board, and is made in metal or plastic.

For heavier-duty fixings choose a plug with flanges that open out and press against the inner face of the board once they have been inserted through a clearance hole. Use extra fixings if you want to increase their holding power.

The strongest fixing for plasterboard

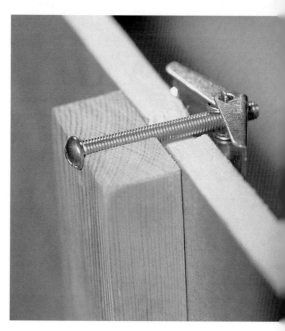

Spring toggles are the strongest type of fixing you can use in plasterboard. The metal arms flip open after the toggle is pushed through a hole in the board. With this version, the toggle is lost if the screw is removed, but some designs have a toggle that remains captive when items are taken down.

SLIDING FIXINGS FOR MIRRORS

Use proprietary mirror clips to fix mirrors without screw holes. The lower clips are fixed, while the upper clips (shown) drop down over the mirror's top edge after its bottom edge has been positioned on the lower clips

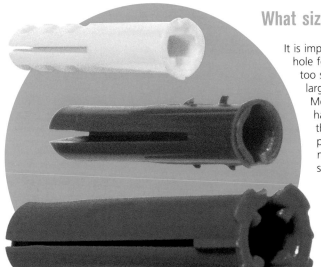

What size plug?

It is important to drill the right size of hole for a plastic wall plug. If it's too small the plug won't fit; too large, and the plug won't grip. Moulded plugs on plastic 'trees' have the drill size stamped on the tree; loose plugs have it printed on the packet. Some manufacturers make different-size plugs in different colours for instant recognition. This is fine so long as you use the same brand of plug all the time, but beware – colours are not standard across different brands.

What size screw?

Screws are specified by two dimensions which are printed on the box or pack – the number or gauge (both terms are used) and the length.

The gauge, or number, is the diameter of the screw's shank, and is not a metric or imperial dimension. The higher the gauge, the bigger the screw.

The length of the screw is still usually given as an imperial measurement on boxes of screws manufactured in the UK. For example, the figures '10 x 2' on the label mean that the screws are gauge or No. 10 and are 2 inches (50mm) long. Screws are also now being sold in a range of metric lengths.

Choose easy drivers

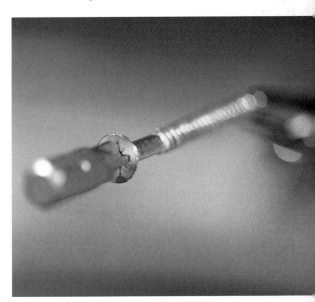

Cross-head screws (Phillips or Pozidriv) are easier to drive than slotted-head types. The tip of the screwdriver engages positively in the recess in the screw head, so there's little chance of the tool slipping and marking the work surface. This is especially important when using a power screwdriver.

Use Pozidriv screwdrivers or bits for driving Pozidriv screws. Choose the No. 1 driver or bit for screws up to gauge 4, the No. 2 up to gauge 10, and the No. 3 for 12 and 14 gauge screws.

Choosing and using nails

The two nail types you are likely to use most frequently are oval wire nails and panel pins. For everyday fixings, keep a supply of these in a compartmentalised storage box.

A stock of nails

There are several types of nail, each in a variety of lengths and with different functions. All are sized in millimetres, and none is expensive. You will want a selection of panel pins, ideal for small repair jobs such as fixing timber mouldings. Useful sizes to keep are 20, 25 and 40mm. Lost-head nails fix panelling to frames; oval wire nails have an oval cross-section and a stubby head, and are the most commonly used nails. Position them with the oval parallel with the wood grain to avoid splitting the wood. Punch in the nail head (see page 34) and fill over it for an invisible fixing. Useful sizes to keep are 50 and 75mm. Round wire nails are used for rough assembly work, such as the framework for a garden pergola. Masonry nails are specially hardened round steel nails, used to fix wood to masonry.

Hammers for maximum impact

A claw hammer, a pin hammer and a club hammer will cater for most household jobs, from tapping in a panel pin to giving a bolster chisel a hefty blow.

If you want a traditional claw hammer with a wood handle, check that the head is securely fixed to it with steel wedges. If you prefer a hammer that's virtually indestructible, choose one with a steel or glass-fibre shaft. Whichever you pick, check whether you can cope with its weight by holding it close to the end of the shaft and swinging it with a smooth, controlled action. It should feel comfortable to use.

Beware of wires and pipes

A cable and pipe detector is a hand-held battery-powered electronic device that will reveal the presence of electricity cables or plumbing pipework concealed in the house structure. It is vital to be aware of their presence whenever you are making fixings into a wall, floor or ceiling, since piercing one could cause personal injury, physical damage or both (see page 28).

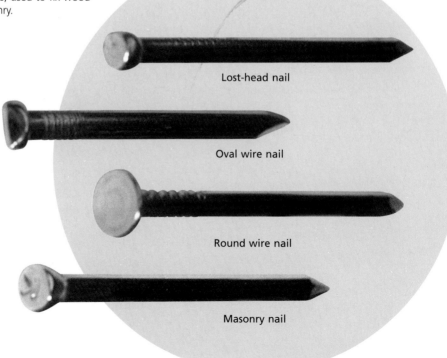

Lost-head nail

Oval wire nail

Round wire nail

Masonry nail

Claw hammer

Pin hammer

Club hammer

Using a claw hammer

A claw hammer will drive all but the smallest nails with ease, and its claw will extract nails that are misaligned or bent while being driven in. Hold it near the end of the handle and watch the hammer head to make sure that it strikes the nail head squarely.

1 Hold the nail between your thumb and forefinger and start it with a few gentle taps of the hammer head. Check that it is at right angles to the surface.

2 Release the nail and drive it in with harder blows. For large nails, keep your wrist stiff and swing hammer and forearm from the elbow. On rough work, hammer the nail head in flush with the surface.

Hammering home

A nail punch

This useful tool lets you drive in nail heads flush with the wood surface without marking the wood with your hammer. Its tip is hollowed out to fit over the nail head. Choose one with a knurled finish for a good grip. A punch with a square head gives you a larger striking surface than a rounded head and is less likely to roll off the edge of your workbench.

Removing a bent nail

If you bend a nail as you drive it, stop and remove it. Do not try to straighten a bent nail or drive it fully home at an angle. Pull it out and replace it with a new nail.

Place a piece of card or thin wood on the surface beside the nail. Hook the hammer claw under the nail head and pull the handle towards you to draw out the nail. Keep the handle vertical so you do not widen the opening of the nail hole.

A professional display

The best hook Always use appropriate picture hooks to hang your pictures. Single-pin hooks will support a glazed frame up to a size of about 900 x 600mm, and a double-pin hook can hang a picture half as big again. Consider using two hooks for larger pictures and mirrors.

Form a group Sets of small pictures look best hung as a group, especially if they share a common theme or are framed in a similar style. Lay the pictures on the floor first, moving them around to experiment with different arrangements. Then measure the overall dimensions of the group and transfer the whole arrangement to the wall.

Single-pin hook

Double-pin hook

MAKING FIXINGS

Putting up curtain poles and tracks

When you move into your new home, give yourself some vital privacy by putting curtains or blinds at the windows. Beg or borrow curtains from friends and family for the time being – you will be able to replace them to match your decor at a later date.

Tools Long wood or metal rule; pencil; bradawl; power drill with wood or masonry bit; screwdriver.

Materials Track/pole plus brackets or sockets, gliders or rings and end stops or finials. Perhaps a length of batten; wall plugs or plasterboard plugs; screws.

Before you start Most tracks or poles must be screwed into sound ceiling timbers or plugs in a wall; extra brackets on ceilings may be screwed into plasterboard plugs. The screws supplied with a track or pole are not always long enough to make secure fixings: replace them if they seem inadequate. Don't saw off any excess track or pole until you are certain there is enough overlap at either end.

Fixing brackets for a track on the wall

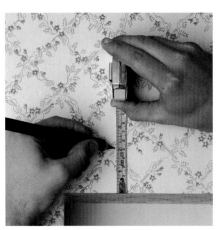

1 Mark the fixing height for the track at least 50mm above the top of the window. Brackets on which a track slots down should be at least 20mm below the ceiling to allow room for fitting the track. Brackets

for clip-on tracks can be up against the ceiling if you wish.

2 Measure up from the window top every 200mm across and make pencil marks at the right height. If the track or pole is to be nearer the ceiling than the window top, measure down from the ceiling. Neither window top nor ceiling is necessarily horizontal. The track should be parallel to whichever of the two is closer or it will always look crooked.

3 Join the pencil marks with a straight line and extend it at the sides to the width of the track. Mark positions for the brackets with pencil crosses on the guide-line. Put one 50mm from each end. Space others about 300mm apart, or as specified in the manufacturer's instructions.

4 At each cross drill through the plaster into the masonry and insert a plug. On a concrete lintel, use a hammer drill. Screw a bracket into each plug.

FIXING TO A CONCRETE LINTEL

Putting up track can be difficult if there is a concrete lintel above the window opening. A solution involving fewer wall fixings and less awkward drilling is to mount a wooden batten on the wall. Drill holes in the lintel with a masonry bit in a hammer drill, then put up the batten with screws and wall plugs and fix the track brackets, which will require many more screws, to this.

Fixing a pole to the wall

1 Draw a guideline on the wall as for fixing brackets for a track on the wall (see opposite).

2 Measure how far above the centre of the bracket the screw hole is and make the drilling marks that distance above the line; 100mm from each end, and in the centre if needed.

Alternatively If the bracket is in two parts, make drilling marks on the guideline through the holes on the mounting plate.

3 Drill and plug the holes. Drive in the screws, letting the heads project; or screw in place the plates for two-part brackets. Fit the brackets in place.

4 Position the pole, centring it on the brackets, and slide on the rings. Make sure that one ring is outside each end bracket and the remainder between the brackets. Push the finials firmly into place at each end of the pole.

5 Drive the screw provided into the hole in the base of each bracket until it bites into the pole. This prevents the pole from being dislodged as you draw the curtains.

HELPFUL TIP

It's important to let as much light as possible into a room, so let the track or pole extend far enough at the sides for the curtains to draw right back, clear of the window.

Fixing brackets in a recess

When fixing a curtain track in a recess, position the brackets as close to the top of the recess as the track and curtains will allow. This will help to avoid light seeping around the top edges of the curtains when they are closed. With a narrow window, the bunched fabric of the curtains when they are open might obscure too much light, so it is worth considering whether a roller blind (page 39) or other kind of blind would be a better option.

1 If the window frame is wooden, screw the brackets directly to it.

2 Where the frame is metal or PVC, screw the brackets upwards into drilled, plugged holes using 38mm No. 6 screws.

Fixing to a window surround

Curtain track

Short batten

Wooden window surround

Windows with wooden surrounds on the wall surface may seem to offer easy fixing points for brackets. However, the track cannot extend beyond the sides of the window. This excludes too much daylight because the curtains cannot be drawn back to clear the glass. Fix a wooden batten at each side of the window to extend the fixing width.

Bending plastic track

Use a hair dryer to warm plastic track where you want to bend it; once warm, it will be more flexible. The tighter the track can be bent to the angles or curves of a bay window, the less room the curtains will take up, although very heavy curtains may tend to 'bunch' if the bend is too tight.

Reusing existing fixings

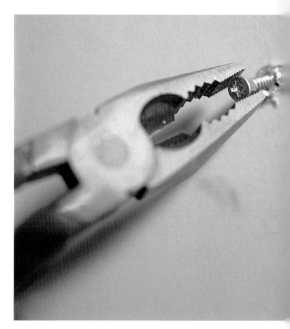

If you are putting back the existing curtain track, after decorating perhaps, check that the old wall fixings are up to the job. Replace frayed or split wall plugs by inserting a screw just far enough to engage in the plug, and then pull the screw and plug out with pliers.

Fit extra-long screws and heavy-duty wall plugs to support track brackets next to cord pulls. It is surprising how much force is exerted on these brackets, especially when you are drawing full-length curtains.

FITTING AND CUTTING TRACK

Put up all the brackets before taking exact measurements for track and cutting it to length. A junior hacksaw is the ideal tool for cutting plastic or metal track. Remove burrs from the track ends with fine abrasive paper to protect your hands from scratches and the curtain material from snags.

Is the track strong enough?

Weigh your curtains before you hang them – get on the scales yourself, then get back on holding the curtains and calculate the difference to get the weight of the curtains. Heavy curtains will need a heavy-duty track. Compare your track with ones in the shop marked as suitable for your curtain weight and replace the track if necessary.

Fitting a roller blind

Roller blinds are a good option for narrow windows, because when open they do not obscure any of the glass, blocking out light. They can be fitted within a window recess or outside it.

Tools *Pencil; power drill with masonry bit for fixing into a wall; screwdriver.*

Materials *Roller blind and brackets; screws for fixing brackets to wall (unless included with the blind); wall plugs (if required).*

Before you start If the window is in a recess, decide whether to fix the blind inside or outside the recess. If inside, measure the full width, from one side of the recess to the other. This will give you the size of the roller blind kit you require. If the blind is to go outside the recess, add 50mm to allow some overlap at either end.

1 Hold each bracket in its position inside the recess as near the top as possible and mark the screw holes for drilling. Make sure the brackets will be level and the same distance from the front of the recess. For a blind outside the recess, make the drilling marks 50mm above the top of the recess, and again make sure that the brackets will be level.

CUT A BLIND TO SIZE

If the exact size of roller you need is not available, buy the next size up and cut it down by sawing the pole and trimming the fabric with scissors.

---

2 Drill and plug the holes, and screw the brackets into place. Then fit the blind by clipping it into the brackets according to the manufacturer's instructions.

Making your own roller blind

You can make a roller blind using fabric of your own choice to get a perfect match with a decorating scheme. Spray aerosol blind-stiffening fluid onto both sides of the material to increase the stiffness of the fabric and to prevent the edges from curling up or fraying.

Stick screws to the screwdriver

Mounting roller blinds at the top of window frames can be tricky because the brackets have to be fitted tight into the corners of the window reveals. The solution is to hold each bracket in place and make the screw holes with a bradawl. Then stick a Pozidriv screw to the blade of your screwdriver with a little Blu-Tack, hold the bracket in place with one hand and drive the screw into its hole with the other.

REVIVING AN OLD BLIND

Through years of use, roller blinds that retract automatically can begin to fail. To increase the tension in the spring of a worn-out roller blind so that it rolls up on its own, pull it down fully and then lift the roller off its brackets. Roll the blind up about half way, replace it on the brackets and test the tension. Repeat the process, rolling up a bit more of the blind each time, until you get the tension right.

Putting it all away

When you first move in to your new home, it may feel as if there's nowhere to put anything. To begin with, try to keep all unpacked boxes in one room, to minimise clutter and stress. Here are some storage ideas.

Wasted space in the bedroom

Double your hanging space Since few items of everyday clothing are ankle length, full-height hanging space in wardrobes is a waste. Convert most of the space you have available to twin-level hanging, with a low-level rail midway between the top rail and the floor.

Raised beds Beds take up a vast amount of valuable floor space. Slide shallow drawers – fitted with castors so they're easy to move – underneath beds on legs. Alternatively, replace existing beds with drawer divans, which have large storage drawers in the bed base, perfect for spare bedding, Christmas decorations, handbags or photographs.

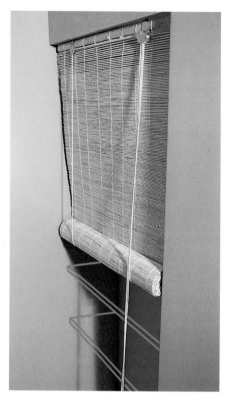

Make use of alcoves Create inexpensive storage by filling an alcove beside a chimney breast with an array of sliding wire baskets, or a set of shelves supported on battens or adjustable track. Then you can hang a roller blind at ceiling level to conceal what's stored behind it.

Simple kitchen ideas

Hang pans from the wall Fix a narrow metal curtain rod with decorative finials to the wall. You can then hang saucepans, spatulas and ladles from S-hooks which are hooked over the rod.

Reuse jars for dried goods Large coffee or mayonnaise jars are ideal for flour, rice and pasta. Kilner jars make good-looking airtight storage for cornflour, icing sugar and muesli. They can simply be ranged along the back of the worktop until you've sorted out your cupboards.

Keep it neat in the bathroom

A bathroom corner If bathrooms have any spare space, it is often in the corners of the room. See if you have space for a floor-standing corner unit that could house both family toiletries and cleaning materials.

Conceal behind the bath panel If you have a homemade bath panel rather than a proprietary plastic moulded one, turn a section of it into a drop-down flap or a removable panel and use it to store bathroom cleaning materials.

What about the door? Make use of the back of the bathroom door with an over-the-door towel rail or towel hooks and use laundry bags on hooks for hiding away toiletries. Or look out for storage racks with suction pads designed for fixing to tiled walls: they will also stick to doors.

Children's rooms

Bunk or cabin beds In a child's room, the bed could be raised to the level of a top bunk, with clothes and toy storage space or a desk built underneath it.

Put the ball in the net Use homemade fabric sacks with drawstring tops or big net bags for storing soft toys, footballs and similar awkwardly shaped things that never seem to stay on shelves or in cupboards. You can hang the bags out of the way on wall hooks or on the backs of room or wardrobe doors.

SAFETY TIP

Tall pieces of furniture, such as bookshelves or wardrobes, should be secured to the wall at the top of the unit, using a bracket or restraining strap. Without them a fully loaded unit could topple over on a child climbing on it or clambering inside.

Maximise space in the garden shed

Recycle old units If you are lucky enough to have a large shed, line the walls with old kitchen units, bookshelves and so forth. This space is invaluable for storing tools, paint and brushes or rollers, buckets, potting compost, garden toys – and if lockable, bikes and power tools.

Use the shed walls Put hooks or nails in the walls for hanging items such as tools and extension cables.

Under-shelf screw store To store small loose items – such as fuses, screws, wallplugs or nails – nail the screw-top lids of jam jars under the shelves. Put the items in the jars and screw the jars into the lids.

Stack and store Buy a range of clear plastic collapsible boxes with lids. You can see what's inside without having to label, mark or open each box before you eventually find what you need; they stack safely and neatly and keep the contents free of dust; and when not in use they can be flattened and stored away.

Self-assembly fixings for flat-pack furniture

When you buy an item of flat-pack furniture, it comes with pre-drilled fixing holes and special types of fixing to enable you to assemble it yourself, with the minimum number of tools.

Often all you need is a special spanner or hex key supplied with the unit. Here are some of the most common fixings that you are likely to encounter.

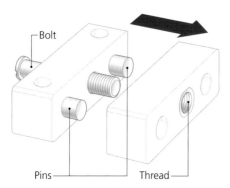

Two block fitting (Lok joint) The joint consists of two plastic blocks and is normally used to join two sections of cupboard together, such as a side to the base. One of the blocks is screwed to the base and the other to the side into pre-drilled holes; a bolt is then screwed in to hold the two sections firmly together. One of the advantages of this type of fixing is that it can be disassembled and reassembled whenever necessary with no loss of strength.

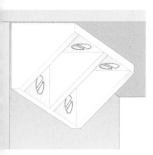

Plastic corner block One of the simplest of the fittings that is often found in flat-pack furniture. Plastic corner blocks hold two panels together at a perfect right angle. As screws are driven into the carcass material, this fitting cannot be taken apart and reused without compromising its strength.

Dowels Dowels are for more permanent joints and those that are not to be taken apart once assembled. Usually about 25–30mm long, they are glued in place. Like the majority of the fixings used in flat-pack furniture they are tapped into factory-made pre-drilled holes. Although simple they are very effective and give a strong concealed joint.

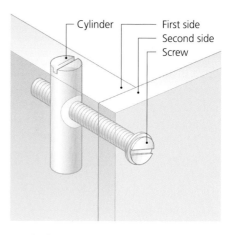

Dowel and screw fitting These are among the most popular joints used in flat-pack furniture. The cylinder is inserted into a factory-made pre-drilled hole in one side of the cabinet. A machine screw is then inserted into a hole in the other side until it meets the cylinder. The two components are tightened with a screwdriver until both sides of the cabinet pull together. The slot in the head of the cylinder part of the fitting allows you to align it so that it will receive the screw (below). Although it is possible to over-tighten these fittings they do hold very securely and can be repeatedly taken apart with no loss of strength.

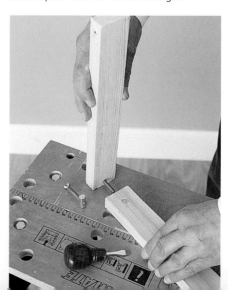

Cam lock fittings

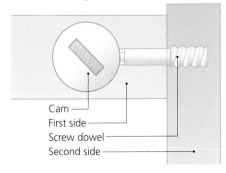

Cam
First side
Screw dowel
Second side

Like the dowel and screw fitting, this fastening is for joining two planks or panels together. The cam is dropped into a shallow recess on the face of one part and a screw with a pronounced head or a steel screw dowel is driven into a pre-drilled hole in the other part to be joined.

The head of the screw passes through a clearance hole in the first part and into the cam. Turning the cam 90° clockwise tightens the joint.

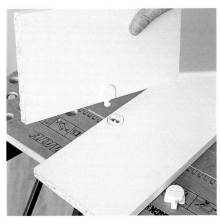

Some cam fittings come with the peg attached to a disc the same size as the cam. Both components slot into pre-drilled holes in the panels to be joined.

Another variation on this type of fitting replaces the peg with a special moulding like a wall plug. This is pushed into a hole drilled in the edge of the second board. A pin is driven into the plug and the fitting is assembled as before.

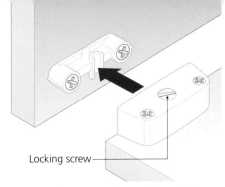

Locking screw

This cam fitting is similar to the Lok joint. The two parts of the joint are screwed into separate panels. The two panels are then brought together and the screw is turned through 90° to lock the joint.

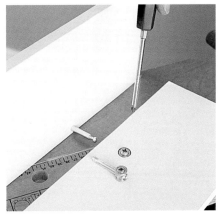

Dowel and bush fitting This fitting consists of a zinc alloy bush and a steel dowel. Screw the dowel into the face of one board so that when it is butt-jointed with the second board it will align with the hole drilled in the second board's edge. The dowel reaches the bush through that hole and is locked in place by turning the grub screw in the bush.

Housing and bolt fitting A bolt screws into the side panel of a cupboard or shelf unit and fits into the housing, which slots into a hole drilled in the underside of the shelf. These fittings are useful for strengthening shelves in an existing unit or for adding extra shelves.

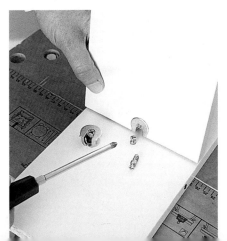

Assembling flat-pack furniture

Whether you are putting together a simple bookshelf, a small bathroom cabinet or a more complex piece of flat-pack furniture, such as a computer desk with a sliding shelf, follow these steps to success.

OPEN WITH CARE

Never use a knife to slit open the packaging as you could damage the panels inside. Lay the pack flat and release the staples, tape or other fixings one by one. Then you can lift out the panels individually, stack them up neatly and retrieve any small bags of fixing devices that may be concealed within the packaging.

1 Unpack the kit and lay out all the components, including the assembly fittings and any other items of hardware such as hinges, handles and feet.

2 Identify all the parts and check that you have the right number of fixings – there is usually a checklist included with the instructions. If any appear to be missing,

look again inside the packaging. If you still cannot locate the missing pieces, return the complete unit to the store and ask for a replacement.

3 Start with the base panel, adding any fixed feet first of all. Build tall units, such as bookshelves or wardrobes, on their backs to make the assembly manageable. If the unit has castors or wheels, fit these last or the unit will keep moving about as you try to assemble it.

4 Connect the first side panel to the base panel. The simplest units have pre-drilled holes through which you can drive screws supplied with the furniture (above). Many units use a combination of glued dowels and cam fixings (pages 42–43). In this case, place the dowels and screwed pegs in the base unit and then offer up the side panel. Glue and locate all the dowels in the side panel, then tighten the fixings.

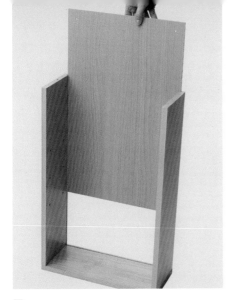

5 Connect the second side panel to make a three-sided box. If the unit has a back panel, locate this in the grooves in the side panels and slide it into place. Then finish the box by fixing the top panel in position.

6 Many fixings come with cover discs that match the colour of the wood or veneer of the finished item. These make a tidy job of disguising the fixings once the furniture is complete. They can be prised out of their holes if you need access to the fixings to dismantle the furniture.

HELPFUL TIP

Much flat-pack and self-assembly furniture comes with a hexagonal assembly key and every unit comes with a set of instructions. When you have finished putting the piece of furniture together, tape the key and instructions securely to the back, so that you will always have them handy if you ever have to move, dismantle or adjust your furniture.

7 Follow the instructions with the unit to add any doors. They will be hung on some form of spring-loaded hinges, and the fitting and fixing holes will all be pre-drilled in the doors and cabinet sides. Fit the hinge body to the door and the mounting plate to the cabinet sides, then connect the two with the short machine screws and adjust them so they hang squarely.

8 Add any shelves, door handles and other internal or external fittings. Double-check that all the assembly fittings are tight, and that you do not have any parts left over. Finally, fit wheels or castors if these are part of the kit.

Building a computer desk

Large items of flat-pack furniture are constructed using special fixings (pages 42–43). Follow the instructions that come with the unit, using these standard techniques to guide you.

Tools Selection of screwdrivers; perhaps a hammer; perhaps a set of hex keys.

Before you start Unpack the box and lay out all the pieces and fixings. Check them against the instructions and make sure that they are all there and you know which piece is which. Often, a right and left hand piece look almost identical until you check where the fixing holes have been drilled.

1 Insert cam lock screw dowels into predrilled holes according to the instructions.

2 Use your thumb to push the cam locks into the large holes on the opposing panels, making sure that the arrow on the fitting points towards the holes on the raw outside edge of the workpiece. The cam lock pins fit into these holes, so if the locks don't face in the right direction the fixings will not work.

WHEN GLUING IS BEST

If you know that you will not be taking the furniture apart again at some time in the future, consider using adhesive on wood-to-wood joints for a sturdier finished piece. Ordinary white PVA wood adhesive is ideal. Use a damp rag to wipe off any excess adhesive that squeezes from the joints.

3 Begin to put the piece together in the order specified in the instructions. In this instance the lock pins are screwed into the cam locks using the special key supplied as part of the kit.

4 This workstation has a sliding keyboard table. The runners for the sliding section are fitted to the keyboard table, and then fixed to the underside of the desk. You will need to turn the desk upside down to make the fixings.

5 Make up the shelf section that sits on top of the desk. This fits onto dowels that have been tapped into the desktop with a hammer. Fit the top to the base and push them together to ensure all the dowels have engaged. If you need to, hammer from above, being sure to protect the workpiece with some scrap timber.

6 Finish the item by adding any accessories. In this instance a simple plastic rack for CDs slots into the narrow stack to the left of the desk.

Putting up shelves

Whether you want to store books, CDs or toys, the most useful solution is custom made shelves. An alcove provides the perfect space, but other options include shelves on fixed brackets, and track systems.

Whatever type of shelving you are putting up, the most important part of the job is getting the shelves horizontal and the brackets and tracks vertical.

Spirit level

You will need a good spirit level. A spirit level has one or more clear vials filled with a liquid. When the level is truly horizontal, a bubble in the liquid floats within an area marked on the centre vial (see page 21).

Laser level

State-of-the-art laser levels fire a laser beam enabling horizontal or vertical guidelines to be marked quickly and accurately.
Laser levels have a wide range of uses including positioning brackets for shelves within an alcove.

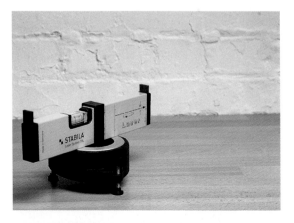

Using a plumb line

A plumb line is simply a weight tied to a length of string. If you hold it firmly at the top, it will hang vertically, provided that the string and weight are not touching anything. You can buy a plumb line, or make your own by tying a heavy nut, or even a small screwdriver, to the end of a length of string.

Tools *Plumb line; a hardback book; a long screw; pencil; a long straightedge, such as a length of track from a shelving system.*

---

1 When fixing shelving track (page 52), mark and then drill the hole for the topmost fixing screw.

2 Plug the hole and partly drive a long screw into it.

3 Suspend the plumb line from the screw so that it hangs as close to the floor as possible.

4 Let the string become steady. Then place one edge of the book on the wall and slide it up to the string until they touch. Mark the wall where the corner of the book has come to rest.

5 Remove the book, string and screw. Using a track from the shelving system or a straight wooden batten, draw a line between the centre of the screw hole and the pencil mark. This line will be the centre line for the track or brackets to be fitted.

6 Other vertical lines on the wall can be measured from the first line, using a steel tape measure. See the table below for guidance on how far apart to set shelf brackets.

BRACKET INTERVALS

Buying the cheapest shelf-and-bracket system can be a false economy if you plan to fill the shelves with heavy loads, such as books. The cheapest shelving material is the weakest, and if it is to be loaded up it will require closer support. This table is a guide to the intervals at which typical shelf materials need to be supported.

15mm chipboard (coated or plain); 15mm softwood (finished thickness)	Heavy loads: brackets at 400mm intervals Medium loads: 600mm intervals
18mm coated chipboard; 18mm MDF; 18mm softwood; 18mm hardwood	Heavy loads: 500mm intervals Medium loads: 700mm intervals
25mm MDF; 25mm softwood; 18mm plywood; 22mm hardwood	Heavy loads: 700mm intervals Medium loads: 900mm intervals
32mm veneered chipboard; 32mm softwood; 25mm plywood; 25mm hardwood	All loads: 900mm intervals

Floating shelves These are so-named because they have no visible means of support. They look modern, clean and attractive, and are great for display purposes. However, they are suitable only for light items. Floating shelves are available in kit form and are supported by a concealed batten or rods fixed into the wall.

Putting up a fixed shelf

Whether for storage or display, fixed shelves must be sturdy, spacious and perfectly level.

Tools Pencil; spirit level; power drill; masonry or wood bit to fit wall plugs; screwdriver. Possibly a straight wooden batten.

Materials Shelf and brackets; screws for fixing brackets to wall; wall plugs to fit screws; small screws for fixing shelf to brackets.

Before you start Check the walls with a battery-powered pipe and wire detector so as not to drill through any hidden pipes or cables (see page 28). You can also use it to detect the positions of the studs (the uprights to which plasterboard is fixed) in a timber-framed wall.

1 Hold a spirit level against the wall at the point where you want the shelf. Check that it is level and draw a light pencil line on the wall. For a long shelf, rest the spirit level on a straight wooden batten.

2 Hold one bracket against the wall with the top against the mark. Use the spirit level to check that it is vertical, and then mark the wall through the screw holes with the pencil.

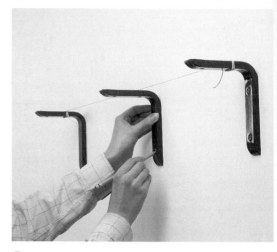

3 Repeat for the second bracket. If there are more than two brackets, it is best to fix the outside ones to the wall, and then tie a piece of string tightly between them across the tops. Then the intermediate brackets can be lined up exactly.

4 Drill holes about 45mm into the wall. Use a masonry bit (or a twist bit if you are drilling into the wooden studs of a light-weight partition wall).

5 Insert plugs into masonry, and screw the brackets tightly to the wall. If the plug turns in the wall as you drive in the screw, remove it, insert a larger one and try again. Do not use plugs in wood.

HELPFUL TIPS

• Right-angled brackets will need screws about 45mm long to fix them to the wall. The screw must go through the plaster and at least 25mm into the brickwork, or into the wood stud if it is a stud partition wall.
• Don't use winged wall plugs to fix brackets to thin hollow walls unless the shelf is only to be used to hold a light decorative object.
• The screws should be the heaviest gauge that the holes in the bracket will take – usually No. 8 gauge on small brackets and No. 10 or 12 on larger ones.

6 Lay the shelf across the brackets. Using a pencil or bradawl, mark the underside of the shelf through the bracket holes.

7 Drill shallow pilot holes for the small screws and screw the shelf into position.

Shelves in alcoves

An ideal place to fit shelves is in an alcove beside a chimney breast. This is best done using wooden battens cut and screwed to the side and rear walls of the alcove.

Positioning the battens

Tools Tape measure; pencil; steel ruler; tenon saw; spirit level; power drill; twist drill bits; masonry bits; countersink bit; screwdriver.

Materials Wood for battens 50 x 25mm; timber or MDF shelves cut to fit alcove; 63mm No. 8 screws and wall plugs; wood filler.

Before you start Cut battens to the length of the back wall and shorter ones to the depth of each shelf. Drill and countersink screw holes no more than 300mm apart through each batten. Battens are fairly unobtrusive even if left square-ended, but to make them less noticeable the ends can be angled or curved.

1 Mark the position of each shelf, checking that the spacing between them is large enough for the items you want to store there – don't forget to allow for the thickness of the shelving material, too.

2 Hold the rear batten to the mark with a spirit level on top. Mark the wall through one end hole with the twist bit. Switch to a masonry bit and drill and plug the hole. Drive in a screw part way.

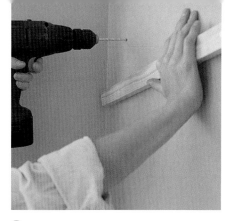

3 Hold the rear batten level and mark the other holes in the same way. Allow the batten to drop out of the way when you drill the wall, then plug the holes and drive the other screws.

4 Position the first side batten, ensuring that it is level with the rear one. Mark the wall beneath it as a guide. Mark drill holes in the same way as for the rear batten. Repeat for the other side batten.

5 Screw the side battens into position. You will be able to hide countersunk screws with wood filler or you could use decorative domed-head brass screws and screw cups.

Fitting the shelves

1 Few walls are true, and your alcove is unlikely to have perfect right angles. Hold a square of card in each internal angle, and if the alcove tapers, cut shelves to the narrower measurement and hide any gaps with beading once the shelves are in place.

2 After you have cut a shelf to fit, drill and countersink a couple of holes through each end and use woodscrews to secure the shelves to the battens.

3 You could strengthen the shelves and improve their appearance by stiffening them with beading fixed along the fronts.

Consider what you will put on your shelves and choose a shelving system that is suitable – overloading shelves is obviously very dangerous.

For heavy loads

Made of steel in lengths from 430mm to 2400mm. Uses brackets from 120mm to 610mm. Available in frost white, black, cream and gloss aluminium. Look for double hooks for extra strength. Accessories may include square book ends, spring rod book supports and universal book supports. Brands include Swish Steel-Lok.

For medium loads

Fully adjustable slot-free systems that can be used for most work around the house. Made of steel in lengths from 188mm to 2500mm. Uses brackets from 100mm to 570mm. Finishes: silver, white, brown, black, red, magnolia, gold and gloss aluminium. Accessories may include book ends, book end shelf supports, end caps, wall plates, clip on shelving supports, a fixing pack and upright connectors. Continuous shelving possible. Brands include Tebrax, Element Single Slot, Element 32 and Swish Design.

For light loads

Easily adjustable, wall-mounted steel shelving systems suitable for light domestic storage. Made of steel in lengths from 500mm to 2000mm. Uses brackets from 125mm to 320mm. Finishes: frost white, black, magnolia. Accessories may include a fixing pack. Brands include Swish Edge Slot.

Adjustable track shelving systems

Track shelving systems consist of tracks which are fixed to a wall, plus brackets which fit into the tracks. Shelves can be raised or lowered by changing bracket positions.

Putting up the tracks

Tools Pencil; power drill; masonry bit; screwdriver; straight wooden batten; spirit level; bradawl.

Materials Tracks and brackets; shelves; screws at least 50mm long to fix tracks to wall; wall plugs; small screws to fix shelves to brackets.

Before you start On a solid wall, you can drive the screws into wall plugs. In a hollow partition wall, locate the vertical studs using a cable and pipe detector (page 28) and screw directly into them.

1 Hold the first track to the wall and mark the position of the top screw with a pencil.

2 Using a spirit level or plumb line, draw a vertical line down the wall the full length of the track (page 48).

3 Measure the position of the other tracks and draw similar vertical lines for each. Once the first vertical has been set, others can be measured off with a tape measure. Tracks are usually placed 700mm apart for 18mm chipboard or timber shelves, and 600mm apart for 15mm shelves (but see also chart on page 49).

4 Use a spirit level to mark the position of the top screw hole on the other vertical lines, level with the first screw position. **Important** Slotted tracks must be fixed at exactly the same height. Otherwise the shelf brackets will not be level.

5 Drill and plug each top screw hole. Screw the tracks temporarily in position, but do not tighten. When they are all in place, check that their tops are level.

6 Use the bradawl or pencil to mark the positions of the other holes on the centre lines. Swing the tracks aside one by one, and drill and plug the holes.

7 Screw the tracks in position. As the screws tighten, watch the track to make certain it is not bending or bowing because of an uneven wall. Pack behind the track with slivers of hardboard or cardboard where hollows occur.

Putting on the shelves

1 Fit the brackets into the correct slots and put on the shelves. Shelves should be slightly wider than the brackets, but avoid wide overhangs which could tempt you to overload the system.

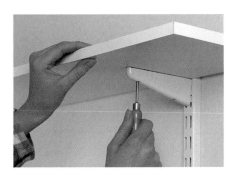

2 Line up the shelves so that their ends are above one another. Mark screw holes in the underside of the shelves by pushing the bradawl through the holes in the brackets.

3 Use the bradawl to make pilot holes and screw the shelves in place. This prevents the shelves from tipping up if anything heavy is put on one end, and stops them from sliding off if they are knocked.

THREE TRACKS FOR FLEXIBILITY

When only two tracks are used, the shelves can be adjusted for height, but each one must run the full width of the system.

Three or more tracks enable shelves to go halfway at one height and the other half at a different height. This allows greater flexibility in storing objects of different sizes. Shelves of different depths can also be used.

Whether two or three tracks are used, the closeness of the shelves in height is restricted by the depth of the bracket plus the thickness of the shelf.

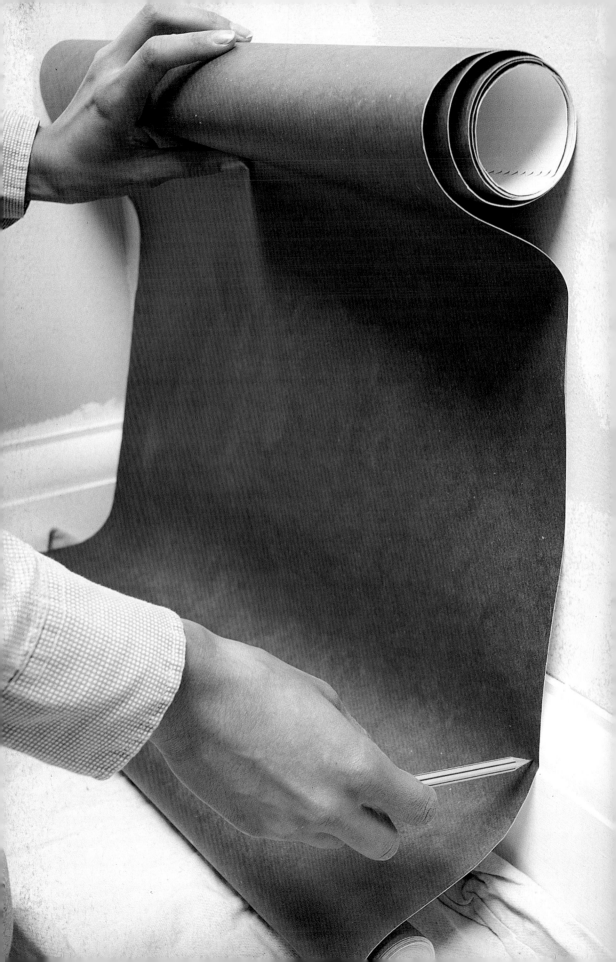

Decorating

Before you paint

Preparation is crucial to a good
decorative finish. There's no point in
spending time and money painting a
room if the wallpaper beneath starts
to bubble, or those carefully glossed
skirting boards chip easily or peel.
Here are the steps you need to take
before you get out the paint brushes.

**Use a steam
stripper** Make
the task of removing
old wallpaper easier and
quicker by using a steam
stripper. A lot of hot
water is generated by the
equipment, so wear
rubber gloves over long
sleeves and protect the
floor well. If you intend
to hire a steam stripper,
it is probably worth
reserving it – they're
always in demand.

Dress for work Protect your skin by
wearing a long-sleeved top, with the cuffs
tucked securely inside a pair of rubber
gloves. Use safety spectacles to protect your
eyes when washing a ceiling.

Protect light fittings
Use plastic bags to
guard ceiling lights
and fans against paint
drips. Make tubes
from stiff paper to slip
over wall lights,
removing shades and
bulbs first.

**Wash with sugar
soap** Clean dirt and
grease off old
emulsion by washing
it with sugar soap
and water. This
solution also takes
the shine off gloss-
painted wood or
metal surfaces, providing a key for the new
coat of paint (see opposite). Wipe with
clean water and allow to dry before
repainting.

Painting over wallpaper You can paint over
wallpaper that is well stuck down. Test
paint on a small area first; if the paper
bubbles, over-painting is not an option.

Score and soak If you have to strip
wallpaper, it is easier if you soften it first.
Score it with a wallpaper perforator or
stripping knife, then soak the surface with
hot soapy water. If you add a handful of
cellulose paste to each bucket of water, it
helps to hold the water on the wall. Then
use a scraper to lift off the paper.

Stripping vinyls Vinyl papers are easier to
strip – the vinyl skin can be pulled from its
backing, then the backing can be soaked
and stripped. With some modern papers
and vinyls, the backing can be left on the
wall as lining paper for a coat of emulsion
(but be sure to test paint a patch first) or
new wallpaper. This only works if the paper
is well stuck. If there are any loose areas,
you will need to strip the whole lot off.

Painting new plaster Even newly
plastered walls need preparation. Let the
plaster dry out completely before
painting. Then prime the highly
absorbent surface with a thin coat of
water-based emulsion diluted to one
part water to four parts paint. Once
dry, the wall is ready to paint.

Textured coatings Thick coatings applied by brush or roller on ceilings and walls are difficult to remove. You could try using a steam wallpaper stripper. Alternatively, try a proprietary textured-paint remover which works like a chemical paint stripper. If you simply want to repaint the textured surface, lightly scrub it with a mild solution of sugar soap and water and allow to dry.

Polystyrene tiles Polystyrene ceiling tiles can be painted with emulsion but never with gloss. Removal is laborious and leaves behind glue that must be scraped off.

Preparing wood and metal

Whether your woodwork or pipework are brand new or old and coated with layers of paint, they will need some preparation before you paint.

New bare wood Apply knotting to all visible knots to stop resin bleeding from them. Look for cracks that need filling. Use fine surface filler (page 58) for interior wood. Smooth using fine abrasive paper, working with the grain. Once preparatory work is complete, apply a coat of wood primer.

Painted wood If paint is sound and in good condition, do not strip it unless the thickness causes an obstruction – making windows hard to open, for instance. Instead, clean with sugar soap and water. This removes dirt and keys the existing paint so that new paint will adhere to it.

Key gloss surfaces Keying – roughening a gloss surface very finely – is essential; without it new paint is easily damaged and scratched off. Where paintwork is slightly damaged but mainly sound, only work on the damaged areas. Rub with a damp flexible sanding pad to remove all loose material, wipe clean and allow to dry. Prime bare wood where it is exposed. Then lightly rub the whole area with very fine abrasive paper and wash with sugar soap, as for sound paintwork. Fill small chips with fine surface filler (page 58).

Dust-free doors and radiators After rubbing down a painted door or radiator with abrasive paper, wipe it with a clean rag dipped in white spirit to remove the dust before applying gloss paint.

Varnished or stained wood Use a chemical paint stripper or varnish remover to get back to bare wood. If stained wood is to be painted and the stain is old, rub down with a flexible sanding pad. If the wood is to be sealed to give a natural finish, remove the stain with a wood bleach. Follow the instructions on the can.

Metal

Aluminium windows and patio doors These do not need painting, but if you want to match a decorating scheme, clean them first with white spirit, dry off and then apply solvent-based gloss paint direct. No primer or undercoat is necessary.

Copper central heating pipes Remove any protective grease with white spirit and rub away any discoloration with fine abrasive paper or wire wool. Wipe clean, then apply gloss or eggshell paint direct. No primer or undercoat is necessary.

Painted metal window frames As with painted woodwork in good condition, do not interfere with sound paint on metal, unless a build-up of paint is making frames too tight. If the paint does not need stripping, clean down the frames with sugar soap and water. Key the surface with fine abrasive paper or wire wool, then apply a primer and gloss paint.

Where rust is lifting paint This may be found in older houses where window frames were not galvanised. Wear safety goggles and brush away flaking paint with a wire brush. Scrape back the remaining paint to reveal bright metal. Do not ignore any hidden rust; it can lead to a new attack. Treat with rust inhibitor, apply a metal primer and paint with gloss.

LEAD IN PAINT

Before the 1960s, paint contained lead. In pre-1960s houses, use a Lead Paint Test Kit to check, as paint with a high lead content can cause lead poisoning. If the surface is sound, paint over it. If you want to strip the paint, wear a face mask that conforms to BS EN149 and open the windows. Use a liquid chemical stripper, put all waste into a sealed bag and consult your local Environmental Health Department for details of safe disposal.

Choosing fillers

A huge range of fillers is available, with new ones being brought out all the time. Here are the main ones.

Hairline crack filler For fine cracks in plaster, plasterboard and painted surfaces.
• Liquid filler applied by brush.
• Dries white in 10 minutes.
• Not suitable on damp surfaces.
• Fully dry in 24 hours.

Paste filler For cracks up to 2mm, small blemishes indoors and gaps in wood. Choose 'fine surface filler' for areas to be gloss painted afterwards.
• Comes ready-mixed in tubes and tubs.
• Can be sanded once dry.
• Surface dry in 30–60 minutes; rapid repair versions dry in 5–20 minutes.

All-purpose filler For cracks and holes in most materials, inside and out.
• Powder or paste; some types are mixed with a diluted adhesive for outside use.
• Dries to a tough, weather-resistant surface that should be painted.
• Do not expose to permanent damp.

Wood fillers Repair cracks and small holes in wood, inside and out.
• Solvent-free paste in tubes and tubs.
• Comes in various wood colours.
• Sets in about 10 minutes; can be sanded, drilled and stained.
• Epoxy-based wood fillers are very strong. Use to any depth; they can be drilled, screwed or planed when dry. The chemically bonded filler and catalyst is quick-setting, so use within 5 minutes.

Frame sealant Fills gaps between masonry and window or door frames.
• Flexible, rubbery paste applied from container fitted into cartridge gun.
• Forms a skin after about 4 hours and can then be painted.
• Available in white and other colours.

Foam filler Largely used for holes or gaps round pipes through a wall – such as where a washing machine drain pipe passes through a kitchen wall.
• Sticky foam applied to dampened surface from pressure spray.
• Expands to 60 times its original volume and moulds to fit shape of hole.
• Expensive but good for awkward areas. Can be cut, sanded and painted when dry.
• Workable for about 5–7 minutes.

Filling small holes and cracks

Small cracks, dents, holes or gouges in plaster walls or ceilings can be repaired with interior filler.

Tools Old paintbrush; filling knife; abrasive paper and block. Possibly also: trimming knife; large paintbrush; plant spray gun; length of wood.

Materials Suitable filler.

1 Rake out the crack with a filling knife. If the crack is in plasterboard and the paper surface has been torn, cut off jagged edges with a sharp trimming knife.

2 Brush the crack with a dry brush to remove dust.

3 Load filler onto the end of the filling knife blade and draw the blade across the crack. Scrape the excess off the blade, then draw it down the crack to remove excess filler from the wall and smooth the surface.

4 For deeper holes, build up the surface in layers, working from the edges. Wait about two hours for each layer to dry before applying the next.

5 When the filler is completely dry, smooth it to the level of the surrounding surface with medium or fine abrasive paper wrapped round a wooden block.

> **HELPFUL TIP**
>
> If the filler pulls away from the wall as you smooth it with your filling knife, try wetting the blade.

Flexible mastic

Gaps between walls and window frames, skirting boards, door frames and staircases, move. Therefore they should be filled with a flexible mastic that sticks well and resists cracking. The mastic is applied with a cartridge gun.

• If the cracks are deep, half-fill them with thin strips of expanded polystyrene before applying the sealant.
• Make sure the sealant reaches to both sides of the gap. Press it in and smooth the surface with a wetted fingertip.

> **HELPFUL TIP**
>
> Instead of licking your fingertip to run along a bead of sealant, dip it in a solution of 50:50 water and washing-up liquid. If you have sensitive skin, use the back of a wetted teaspoon instead or wear latex gloves.

Using wood filler

The type of wood filler you choose depends on whether the wood is going to be waxed or varnished or hidden under a coat of paint.

Wood must have a well-prepared surface before the final finish is applied. This means filling any holes before the wood is finally sanded smooth. If the wood is to be left its natural colour, buy a wood filler that matches. If it is going to be painted, fill with an interior filler.

Tools Filling knife; abrasive paper.

Materials Interior filler or wood filler.

1 If you plan to paint the wood, sand it with fine abrasive paper to key existing paintwork. Then wash it with a solution of hot water and sugar soap (page 57).

2 If you are repainting the area, use interior wood filler to fill any defects such as cracks or dents. Be sure to press the filler in firmly and scrape away any excess.

3 Once the filler has set hard, sand it smooth ready for painting.

4 If you intend to apply a finish through which the wood can be seen – stain, wax or varnish – then sand it smooth and fill it with a wood filler (also known as stopping) that matches the colour of the bare wood as closely as possible.

5 Press the stopping into the holes and cracks, taking care not to spread it into the surrounding grain.

6 Wait until the stopping has dried to the same colour all over – usually about 30 minutes – then sand it flat.

Filling an open woodgrain

If a wooden door has a very open grain, and you want to achieve a smooth painted finish, you will need to work in a paste of fine-surface filler. Apply the filler with a flexible filling knife, pushing it right into the grain. Then wipe away the excess with a damp rag.

Choosing paints

Before you buy paint study colour charts or, better still, buy some tester pots to try out on the wall. Paint tends to look darker once it is applied, so if you are doubtful about which shade to buy, choose the paler one.

Think about your furniture, curtains and accessories, and aim to unify the room with colour. When trying out a tester pot, paint a square on two walls – you will be surprised at the difference that varying levels of natural light make to a colour.

How much paint do you need?

Work out how much paint you need before you buy any at all. It's better to overestimate than underestimate, so as to be sure that you can complete an entire room with paint from the same batch.

COVERAGE PER LITRE

Coating	Coverage
Primer	8–12m^2
Undercoat	16m^2
Gloss	14m^2
Non-drip gloss	12m^2
Emulsion	10–13m^2

Most paint tins indicate the average area of wall or other surface they will cover, but this table (above) offers a rough general guide for different types of paint. Porosity, texture and the base colour of the surface will affect the amount you actually need. Highly porous surfaces, such as bare plaster, will absorb a considerable amount – especially when priming. Textured surfaces, such as woodchip, are also very thirsty. You made need to apply two or three coats if you are painting over a bold base colour.

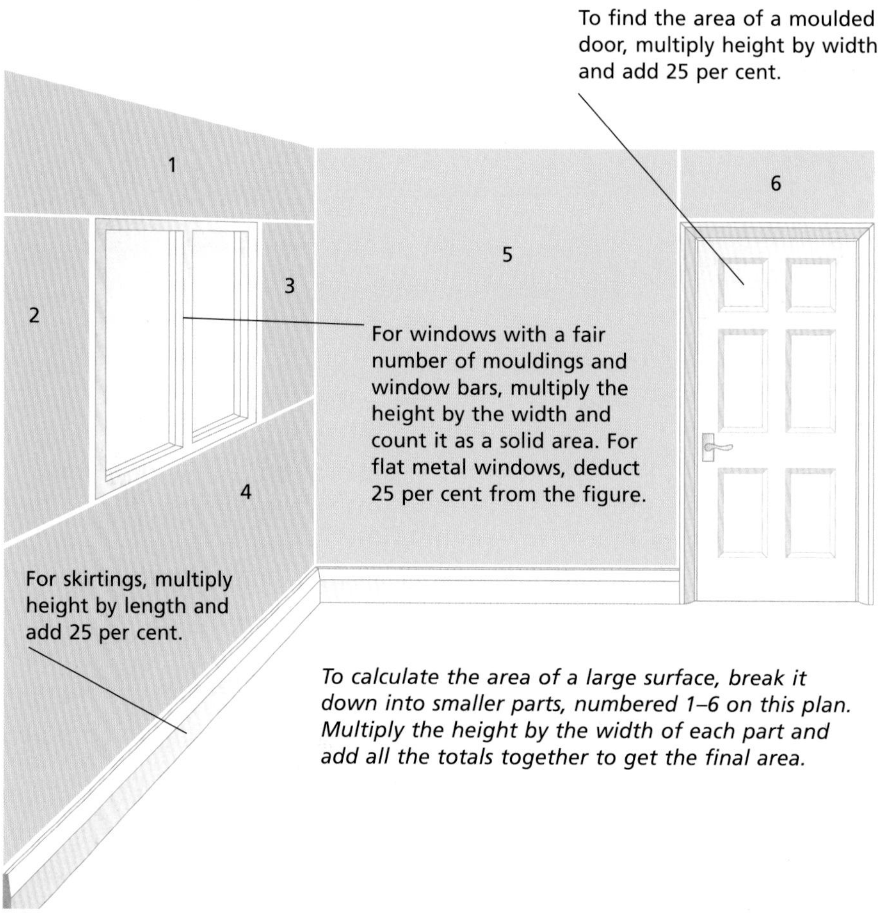

To find the area of a moulded door, multiply height by width and add 25 per cent.

1

6

5

3

2

4

For windows with a fair number of mouldings and window bars, multiply the height by the width and count it as a solid area. For flat metal windows, deduct 25 per cent from the figure.

For skirtings, multiply height by length and add 25 per cent.

To calculate the area of a large surface, break it down into smaller parts, numbered 1–6 on this plan. Multiply the height by the width of each part and add all the totals together to get the final area.

Common types of paint

Water-based emulsions, in either silk or matt finish, are used for walls and ceilings. Choose solvent-based paint, or gloss, for woodwork or metal.

HELPFUL TIP

Don't stir non-drip paint, even if it looks lumpy in the tin. If the paint becomes liquid because it has been accidentally stirred or shaken, leave it to re-set before using.

Solvent-based paint must be used with an undercoat, but this is not necessary for emulsion. You can also buy water-based gloss paints. They are faster to dry and easier to clean, but tend to give a less glossy finish.

Jelly-like non-drip paints are ideal for less experienced decorators, as they don't run. They may be more expensive per litre, but seldom need an undercoat or second topcoat, so may not cost any more in the long run.

The final coat of paint – the topcoat – can have a gloss, semi-gloss or matt finish. Other names for semi-gloss include eggshell, silk, satin and sheen. The glossier the paint, the tougher and more durable the surface will be. Also, look out for moisture-resistant paints developed for kitchens and bathrooms.

Undercoat
• A full-bodied paint with more pigment than topcoat and good covering power.
• Used on primed surfaces, before applying topcoat, or on dark surfaces which are to be painted a paler colour.
• Apply a second coat if undercolour shows through the first coat.
• Wash brushes with white spirit.

Solvent-based gloss
• Used for woodwork and metalwork. Gloss is suitable indoors and out.
• Can also be applied to walls and ceilings.
• On wood, always use with an undercoat.
• Apply two thin coats, rather than one thick one.
• Clean brushes with white spirit.

Non-drip or one-coat paint
• Used for interior woodwork.
• Combines undercoat and topcoat and stays on the brush well.
• Two coats may be needed when covering a dark colour.
• Clean brushes with white spirit.

Water-based gloss
• Used for woodwork and furniture.
• Dries much faster than solvent-based gloss.
• Gives a glossy, hardwearing finish.
• Clean brushes with water and detergent.

Emulsion
• Water-based paint used for walls and ceilings.
• Dries quickly and does not leave brush marks.
• Can be diluted with 20 per cent water to form its own primer for bare plaster.
• Use a roller for fast coverage.
• Two or three coats may be needed.
• Clean tools with water and detergent.
• Solid non-drip emulsion, sold in wide shallow trays designed to take a standard decorating roller, is ideal for ceilings.

Anti-condensation paint
• The best paint to use in bathrooms and kitchens as it will not peel away when exposed to a lot of steam.
• A semi-porous emulsion which absorbs moisture in the air and allows it to evaporate as the air dries.
• Will not cure condensation, only reduce its effect on the painted surface by preventing droplets forming on the surface.
• Often contains fungicide to deter mould.
• Apply in the same way as emulsion.
• Clean tools with water and detergent.

Enamel paint
• Used for metal and wood, especially children's toys and furniture.
• Non-toxic.
• No primer or undercoat needed.
• Clean brushes with white spirit.

Other special paints
• Matt black is used for beams and blackboards.
• Radiator enamel stays white when hot.
• Anti-damp paint seals in minor surface dampness.
There are also special paints for floors, garage floors, tiles and melamine (for brightening up old kitchen units).

Tools and tips for putting on paint

There are several options when it comes to applying paint. Rollers are a good choice for large areas such as walls and ceilings. Brushes come in a variety of shapes and sizes to suit every paint job.

Choosing a roller

It's worth buying a good-quality paint roller, with a cage that spins freely and springs back into position when you squeeze it. Look for a comfortable handle, with a threaded insert to take an extension pole. The pole will save you bending if you want to paint a floor, or climbing a stepladder to reach ceilings. A telescopic pole is the most versatile type.

Use a cheap foam roller sleeve for general painting work where the standard of the finish is not important. For a good finish on a very smooth surface, a mohair sleeve with a short pile is best. A sleeve with a long lambswool or synthetic fibre pile forces paint into every crevice on a highly textured surface, such as woodchip.

Reaching behind a radiator

Use a radiator roller or brush to paint behind a radiator. Both tools have long handles, so the new paint colour can be taken right out of sight. Be sure to remove dust and cobwebs before you start.

Choosing a brush

A cheap brush is fine if a good finish isn't important – when brightening up an understairs cupboard, for example. Try to use the brush for priming and undercoating first, so that when it's time to apply the top coat it has stopped shedding bristles.

Modern synthetic fibre brushes will perform as well as all but the finest hog bristle brushes, and suffer far less from 'hair loss' in use. They are also easier to clean than bristle brushes, and keep their shape better too.

What size brush?

The general rule is to use the widest brush that you can handle comfortably, and which is appropriate for the surface being painted. A 100mm brush is ideal for applying emulsion paint to walls, while a 75mm one is better for gloss-painting flat woodwork The wider the brush, the quicker you can paint, making it easier to keep a wet edge as you work. Cutting-in brushes have a slanted end, making it easier to reach neatly into angles and corners.

Cutting-in brush   50mm brush

100mm brush

150mm brush

Using a pad

A paint pad is a good choice for applying thin coats of emulsion to smooth surfaces. They can also be used with solvent-based paints, and cleaned in white spirit.

Painting bare plaster

Dilute emulsion using one part water to four parts paint. It will be very runny, so cover everything you don't want spattered – including yourself. Apply this priming and sealing coat with a foam or mohair roller and do any touching up with a small brush while the paint is still wet. Follow with at least two coats of full-strength emulsion.

Keeping mould at bay

Steamy kitchens and bathrooms can be ideal breeding grounds for mould, because of the condensation that forms on wall and ceiling surfaces. Decorate them with special kitchen and bathroom paint (see page 61).

Pick healthier paints

Water-based paints and varnishes have a lower volatile organic compound (VOC) content than solvent-based ones. This means they do less environmental damage and pose less of a health risk to people using them regularly. Use products with a low VOC rating if solvent-based paints give you nausea or headaches. Information about VOCs is often given on the container.

Textured coatings

Use a brush or shaggy pile roller to apply paint to a textured surface, such as Artex or woodchip. You will find that emulsion gives the best results. Textured coatings are sometimes abrasive so they may rip foam rollers and be difficult to coat thoroughly.

To create a textured finish on a smooth wall, use a sculptured roller sleeve. Hessian, bark, swirl, patchwork and stipple effects are among those available. Some can be used to create a repeating pattern with successive parallel passes of the roller.

Painting walls and ceilings

To avoid spattering newly painted surfaces with drips, paint the ceiling first, then the walls and finally the woodwork. It is a good idea to paint the ceiling (which can be a messy job) before stripping any wallpaper. But this is the only exception to the rule that all preparatory work must be done before you start painting.

Painting a ceiling

Make sure that you can safely reach the area you are decorating. Use a scaffold board supported by trestles or stepladders. Your head should be about 75mm from the ceiling. Alternatively, use an extension handle (or broomstick) fitted to the hollow handle of a roller, for most of the painting. You will need to stand on steps or a board to cut-in where the walls and ceiling meet.

Paint the ceiling in strips starting near the window (or the window that lets in the most light, if there is more than one). Cut in the edges as you work.

WHEN TO PAINT COVING

If you paint coving and ceiling roses after you have painted the ceiling, you will avoid getting splashes on the new paintwork. If coving is to be the same colour as the ceiling, paint it before you paint the walls; if not, paint it after the walls.

Painting with emulsion

1 Start at the top of the wall. Apply the paint in all directions, working horizontally across the surface and moving down when one band is complete. Do not put the paint on too thickly.

2 Lay off the paint with light brush strokes and a fairly dry brush, working in a criss-cross pattern. Lift the paint finally on upward strokes.

Using a brush

A paintbrush is a versatile tool for applying primers, undercoats and varnishes, as well as topcoats to a variety of surfaces. Use one for applying gloss to wood and metalwork and for painting where colours or surfaces meet – around windows and doors, for instance.

1 Stir the paint – unless it is non-drip. Make sure any liquid on the surface is thoroughly mixed in.

2 Choose the right sized brush. As a rough guide, paint window frames with a 25mm brush, door panels with a 75mm brush, and walls and other large surfaces with a 100mm brush. Grip large brushes around the handle and hold smaller brushes more like a pencil.

3 Flick the bristles against your hand to remove dust and any loose bristles or dried paint particles.

4 Dip the brush into the paint, to about one-third of the bristle depth, to load it with paint.

5 Press the brush against the paint tin or kettle wall to remove surplus paint. Do not scrape the brush over the rim because too much paint will come off.

Painting a textured surface

When painting a surface with a heavy texture or relief, load the brush with more paint than for a smooth ceiling or wall. This cuts down the time it takes to coat the surface and fill all the little indentations. But dip to only a third of the bristle depth. If you are painting a relief wallpaper,

Anaglypta for example, use a brush as wide as you can comfortably manage without putting too much strain on your wrist. With a textured coating on a wall or a ceiling, you can use a shaggy pile roller.

HELPFUL TIP

Line a paint kettle with aluminium foil – to make cleaning easier – and pour in paint to fill about one-third of the kettle. Do not work from the tin; you may contaminate the paint with dried paint, dirt and possibly rust from around the rim.

Using a roller

You can cover an area more quickly with a roller than with a brush, but you may need to apply more coats because the paint goes on quite thinly. Use a foam or mohair pile on a smooth surface and a lamb's-wool or nylon pile on a textured one.

1 Thoroughly stir the paint (unless it is a non-drip or solid roller paint).

2 Fill about one-third of the roller tray with paint. Do not overfill, or it will spill.

3 Dip the roller into the paint, then run it lightly on the ridged part of the tray. This spreads the paint evenly on the roller sleeve.

4 Push the roller backwards and forwards, alternating diagonal strokes at random.

5 Do not apply too much in one coat. And do not work too fast, or paint will be thrown off the sleeve and spatter. Try not to press the roller too hard or paint will be forced off the ends in ridges.

USING NON-DRIP PAINT

Do not stir non-drip paint and do not remove any excess paint from the brush; it is meant to be heavily loaded. Apply the paint in horizontal bands. Don't overbrush or the paint will run.

6 Use a small paintbrush to cut in the edges around doors, windows, corners and where walls meet the ceiling.

Cutting in

Achieve a neat finish along wall and ceiling edges by first painting the edges with a brush, before switching to a roller or pad. Paint four or five overlapping strokes at right angles to the edge. Then cross-brush over the painted area in a long, sweeping motion, keeping parallel with the edge.

Beading where colours meet

Where walls meet the ceiling and where adjacent walls are of different colours, keep the meeting edge as straight and as neat as possible. Do not rush the job.

1 Turn the paintbrush edge on, holding it like a pen, and load the brush with enough paint to cover about one-third of the bristle depth.

2 Press the brush flat against the surface so that a small amount of paint (the bead) is squeezed from the bristles. Work towards the edge gradually, rather than trying to get close immediately.

3 Draw the brush sideways or downwards along the surface, keeping your hand steady.

Keep equipment as good as new

If you look after brushes and rollers, and store leftover paint carefully, you will save money, and be able quickly and easily to touch up any damage.

You can stop a loaded roller from drying out by sliding a plastic bag over the sleeve; squeeze out the air and secure the neck of the bag with a wire tie.

Storing rollers Make sure a roller sleeve is completely dry before storing it. Then wrap it in brown paper or polythene and tie up the ends to keep it clean.

Keep bristles shapely Wrap polythene around the bristles of cleaned brushes, secure with rubber bands, and hang them from hooks or nails. Next time you need to use them, your brushes will be clean and, most importantly, the bristles won't be misshapen.

Overnight break When you take a break during painting, wrap your paintbrush tightly in either kitchen foil or cling film so air cannot get to it. The brush will then be ready for use later – or even the next day.

Cleaning off water-based paint

When you finish using a water-based paint, clean as much of it as possible off brushes and rollers so that as little as possible is washed down the drain. Use the back of a knife and work from the base of the bristles to the tip. Then wipe on newspaper. Finally, rinse the roller sleeve or bristles in running water so as to dilute the paint before it enters the drains.

Give an old brush new life

Before reusing a poorly stored brush, flick the bristles against your hand to remove any dust or hardened bits of paint. Try removing any remaining paint with an old comb. Then restore life to the bristles by soaking the brush in a solution of water and hair conditioner, or a proprietary brush restorer.

Best ways to store and dispose of paint

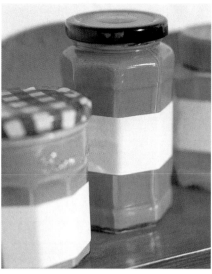

Store leftovers in jars

A small amount of paint will keep better if you decant it from the tin into a jar with a screw-top lid. Make sure you have enough paint to fill the jar, or a jar small enough to just take the paint, so there's little room for air. Rub some petroleum jelly around the neck of the jar before pouring in the paint; then any that spills down the outside won't make the lid stick fast. Remember to label the jar for future reference.

Dealing with oil-based paint

Scrape excess paint off the bristles using the back of an old knife. Then clean solvent based paint from bristles or roller sleeves by washing them in white spirit decanted into a jar or tin.

Never pour used white spirit or solvent-based paint down the sink or into a drain. It's best to consult your local authority about getting rid of any solvent-based product; the environmental services may have special disposal facilities.

Recycle white spirit

Save money and the environment by recycling white spirit after using it to clean brushes and rollers. Let the paint residue settle in the spirit container, then strain the clear solvent off into a clean container with a child-proof lid and label it clearly. Wrap up the hardened paint residue and the dirty container in newspaper before putting them in the dustbin.

Use a piece of kitchen foil to prevent a skin forming on the top of an opened tin of paint. Using the lid as a guide, cut a circle of foil large enough to cover the surface of the paint. Press it down gently to exclude air trapped beneath it. Alternatively, you can stop a skin from forming by tipping a tin of paint upside down before storing. The paint flows around the underside of the lid to form an airtight seal when the tin is turned the right way up again. Don't store the tin upside down – a skin will simply form below the paint.

Unwanted water-based paint can be sealed in its tin and put out for the refuse collectors.

Painting woodwork

Once the ceiling and walls are painted, move on to the woodwork. Whatever the surface, the order of painting remains the same.

Tools Paintbrushes; abrasive paper; wood sanding block; thin piece of wood; dusting brush; lint-free cloth.

Materials Wood filler; knotting; primer; undercoat; topcoat.

1 Brush a coat of knotting over any resinous areas or knots in the wood so they are sealed and resin cannot seep through.

2 Apply an even coat of primer to bare wood and leave it to dry.

3 Rub lightly over primed areas with fine grade abrasive paper wrapped around a block of wood. Sand moulded areas as well. Use abrasive paper round a thin piece of wood, or a flexible sander.

4 Put one undercoat on light surfaces and two on dark ones.

5 When the undercoat is dry, gently rub with abrasive paper. Remove dust with a dusting brush. To pick up remaining dust, wipe with a damp lint-free cloth.

6 Apply the topcoat with a brush that is an appropriate size for the surface.

FOR A PERFECT FINISH

To avoid a disappointing final appearance, sand wood smooth and fill any holes before painting.

1 Wrap a piece of abrasive paper around a wood sanding block and rub it along the grain of the wood.

2 Then remove all the dust, with a fine brush, brushing in the direction of the grain to clear all crevices.

3 Press wood filler into holes, taking care not to spread it into the surrounding grain.

4 Wait until the filler has dried – perhaps 15–30 minutes – then sand it flat and dust once more.

Painting doors

Doors have several faces and grain patterns going in different directions, each of which needs to be painted separately in a particular sequence for a good finish. Always open a door before you paint it. Leave the door frame until last.

Tools Suitable brushes; perhaps cutting-in brush; paint shield.

Materials Masking tape; wire wool; white spirit; knotting; primer; undercoat; topcoat.

Before you start Take off any door furniture, put down a dust sheet and hold the door open with a wedge on either side. It's a good idea to keep the door handle nearby in case the door closes.

Panelled doors

Paint the sections of the door in the sequence illustrated (facing page), for best results.

Use a brush of a suitable size to paint each part of the door – use a smaller one for the mouldings than for the panels, for instance.

Do not overload the mouldings with paint; this is a common cause of drips and runs. Keep the brush lightly loaded.

Glass panelled doors

Use a paint shield, an angled cutting-in brush (page 62) or masking tape to keep paint off the glass. Whichever you use, allow paint to bleed onto about 2mm of the glass to seal where the glass and frames meet.

Paint the rest of the door with a broader brush – about 75mm wide. To avoid drips, do not overload the brush with paint.

If gloss paint gets on the glass, remove it with a rag damped with white spirit before it dries. If paint dries on the glass, scrape it off with a glass scraping tool.

IF THE WALLS ARE TO BE PAPERED

If a room is to be papered, overlap paint onto the wall around door and window frames, above skirting boards and below picture rails.

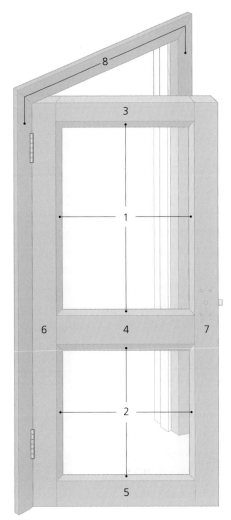

Panelled doors Paint the panels and the mouldings, then the rest of the surfaces.

Glass doors Paint the moulding around the glass before the remainder of the door.

Painting wooden mouldings

Skirting boards and picture rails are usually painted with gloss to match any other painted woodwork in the room. Balustrades are painted to match doors and other woodwork in the hall. If the walls are to be papered, paint woodwork first.

Tools *Suitable brushes; pieces of old card.*
Materials *Paint; white spirit.*

Before you start Fill damaged woodwork with fine surface filler then rub down to give a smooth finish ready for painting – gloss paint will show up every dent.

Skirting boards

If you can, lift fitted carpets before painting a skirting board. When the carpet cannot be lifted, protect it with dust sheets or a piece of card held beneath the brush.

1 The gap between the skirting board and the floor is likely to be full of dust. To remove the worst of it, vacuum along the skirting board before beginning. Then use a piece of card to stop the paintbrush from touching the floor.

2 Apply paint with a 50mm or 75mm paintbrush, depending on the height of the skirting board. Brush lengthways along the run of the board.

Picture rails

1 With a 25mm brush, paint two or three thin coats, not one thick one, allowing each coat ample time to dry.

2 Finish off with fine brush strokes along the run of the picture rail.

Painting interior windows

It nearly always takes more time to paint a window than you think, because of the number of surfaces and because you have to keep paint off the glass. For security reasons, you will probably want to close windows at night, so start work as early in the day as possible.

Tools *25mm or 50mm brush or an angled cutting in brush (page 62).*

Materials *Masking tape; wire wool; white spirit; primer; undercoat; topcoat; cling film or talcum powder.*

Before you start Put down dust sheets, and protect the glass with masking tape. Fix the tape about 2mm from the frame so that a thin line of paint goes onto the glass. This will seal any gap between the glass and the frame. Or use a masking shield, moving it along as you paint and cleaning it regularly.

Casement frames

1 Open the window. Paint the frame in the order illustrated below. Do not apply too much paint in one coat or it will run and take longer to dry.

2 The painting sequence is largely determined by the fact that the brush strokes should follow the construction of the joinery; so the vertical brush strokes will 'cut off' the horizontal ones.

3 Keep paint off handles and stays. These look best cleaned up and left natural. Remove any dried paint splashes on metal with wire wool dipped in white spirit.

4 If you have to close casements and the paint is touch-dry but not absolutely hard, rub a little talc on the meeting surfaces. Alternatively, place a sheet of cling film between the surfaces most likely to stick.

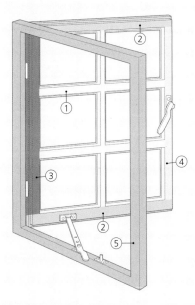

Order of work
Paint casement windows in this order:
1 cross-bars and rebates; **2** top and bottom cross-rails; **3** hanging stile and hinge edge; **4** meeting stile; **5** frame. The colours on the drawing indicate the extent of the numbered areas.

Sash windows

1 Paint the frame following the order shown below. Almost close the window to paint the inside runners; give them a very thin coat to prevent surfaces from sticking.

2 Do not paint the sash cords or they will harden and fail earlier than they should.

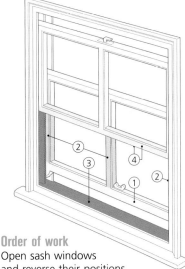

Order of work
Open sash windows and reverse their positions, then paint in the following order:
1 meeting rail; **2** vertical bars as far as possible; **3** the area that the inner sash sits on, and lower runners; **4** cross-rail and underside.

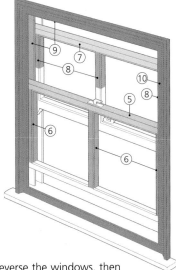

Reverse the windows, then paint: **5** cross-rail; **6** vertical bars; **7** cross-rail; **8** rest of vertical bars; **9** soffit, top runners and behind cords; **10** frame. Colours indicate the extent of the numbered areas.

PAINTING WOODWORK

Painting metalwork

Make sure that all metalwork is clean and free from grease before painting.

Radiators

Never paint a hot radiator – always let it cool first. Wait for about an hour after you finish painting, then turn on the heating to speed up the drying process. Special radiator paint is available that will keep its whiteness despite the heat.

Before you start Check for patches of rust or bare metal that may be showing through. Rub them down with a fine wet-and-dry abrasive paper, and then touch them up with metal primer.

1 Apply gloss direct to new and already painted radiators unless there is to be a colour change, in which case apply an undercoat first.

2 Use a 50mm brush and keep the coat as thin as possible to avoid runs. You can paint a flat panel radiator with a small roller; this will not give quite as good a finish, but takes less time than painting with a brush.

3 Do not paint over control valves; they must be left free to turn.

Painting metal pipes

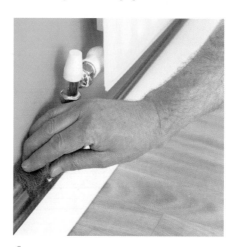

1 Make sure that steel and copper pipes are clean and free from corrosion. Use fine wire wool to clean them.

2 Apply gloss paint direct with a 25mm or 50mm brush. There is no need for a primer unless the pipe is lead. Start by brushing up and down, then smooth the paint along the length of the pipe.

3 Never paint over stop taps or controls or they will not work.

Metal windows

Don't let paint layers build up on metal windowframes, as they tend to be tight fitting. If paint layers are very thick, remove the paint with a chemical stripper. Then paint following the order as for wooden frames (page 71).

Dealing with paint problems

The main causes of paint breaking down are incompatible paints being applied on top of one another, poor preparation of the surface, damp or trapped moisture, grease, rot or rust.

Blistering Prick a blister – if water emerges, damp is trapped under the paint or is finding its way in from behind.
• Strip the blistered paint with a hot-air gun and leave the wood until it has dried.
• Prime the surface and then repaint the whole of the repaired area.

Visible under-colour Liquid gloss does not have good covering power, so always use undercoat to hide a strong colour.
• Put on another layer of topcoat, but switch to a one-coat paint, which has more body and covering power.

Runs Too much paint applied in a thick coat results in runs that are hard to disguise.
• If the paint is still wet, brush out runs; but not if the paint has started to dry. Instead, wait until it is completely dry and then rub down with very fine abrasive paper until the surface is smooth.
• Clean with a damp rag.
• Apply a new thin topcoat.

Mould and discoloration Mould patches are often due to condensation.
• Treat the affected area with a fungicide as directed by the manufacturer, wash the surface clean, let it dry and then repaint.

Loss of gloss sheen Gloss paint will sink into the surface and lose its shine if the surface was not primed – or if either primer or undercoat was not left to dry completely.
• Rub down with damp wet-and-dry abrasive paper.
• Brush off the dust and wipe with a clean, damp rag, then apply a new topcoat.

Dark patches on painted wood Knots in wood which have not been sealed before you decorate may ooze resin when the sun warms them, and the resin will force its way through the paint film.
• Strip paint away with the edge of a scraper blade, then with fine abrasive paper to expose the knot.
• Brush knotting (page 68) over the area to seal it, leave it to dry and repaint.

Dropped bristles Unless you spot a stray bristle as soon as it appears and can lift it off the paint before it gets stuck, wait until the surface is thoroughly dry before trying to remove it. Then carefully cut it away with a scalpel or sharp craft knife.

Wrinkled paint Usually caused by applying a second coat of paint before the first has dried. Solvents in the wet paint underneath attack the second coat when they try to pass through it and make it wrinkle.
• Strip the paint with a chemical stripper or hot air gun and redecorate, allowing each coat to dry before applying the next.

Gritty paint surface If a newly painted surface feels rough and gritty, paint has been applied with a dirty brush or has become contaminated by the surrounding areas. Or there may have been bits of skin in the paint. Strain old paint through a paint strainer or a pair of tights. Use a paint shield or piece of card to guard against picking up dirt from a floor.
• When a gritty surface is dry, rub smooth with damp wet-and-dry abrasive paper, wipe clean, then apply a new coat of paint.

Paint spills Act fast if you spill paint. Scrape up as much as you can with a flat-bladed tool. Then dab off what's left with dry absorbent cloths and paper before lifting the last traces with clean cloths dampened with cold water (for spilt emulsion) or white spirit (for solvent-based paint). Use washing-up liquid on a damp cloth to remove all traces of white spirit from carpet pile or fabric.

Paint will not dry The room is badly ventilated or very cold.
• Open all the windows and doors or put a heater in the room.
• If this does not solve the problem, the paint has been applied to a dirty – and probably greasy – surface.
• Strip it off with chemical stripper or heat and start again, taking great care to clean the surface thoroughly.

Paint on glass The best tool for removing paint from a window pane is a plastic scraper fitted with a trimming knife blade. The blade should be inset very slightly so it cannot mark the frame.

Choosing wallpaper and paste

Duplex paper The top surface – often with a relief pattern – is bonded to a backing paper. It is strong, easy to hang and holds its shape. Easier to hang than other relief wallpapers.
Paste Use all-purpose, cold-water, heavy-duty or ready-mixed.

Paste-the-wall papers Available in a wide range of colours and designs. They are easy to hang (and strip off) and can be wiped clean.
Paste Use all-purpose, cold-water or ready-mixed and apply to the wall, not the paper.

Relief wall coverings Heavy papers, such as Anaglypta, embossed with a pattern during manufacture. Suitable for uneven walls and ceilings. Can be painted.
Paste Use all-purpose, cold-water or ready-mixed.

Vinyl PVC layer, with pattern or texture, bonded to paper. Durable and washable.
Paste Use all-purpose or ready-mixed (both with fungicide) or vinyl adhesive.

Choosing paste
• Use a paste recommended by the manufacturer of the wall covering you have chosen. In general, the heavier the wall covering, the stronger the paste will need to be.
• Many pastes can be mixed to different strengths to suit standard wallpaper or heavy vinyls by adding more or less water. Follow the instructions on the packet.
• Many wall coverings must be left to one side for a time after they have been pasted to allow the paste to soak into the paper. The paper expands slightly when it is damp and if it is not left to soak it will continue to expand on the wall, making matching difficult and perhaps forming bubbles. In general, heavy thick coverings need to soak for longer than thin ones. Vinyls need no soaking time because vinyl does not expand when damp.

All-purpose paste For all wall coverings. Powder or flakes are mixed with varying quantities of cold water to suit the particular wall covering. Follow the instructions on the packet. Contains a fungicide. Water content varies between 4–7 litres per sachet, covering 2–10 rolls.

Lining paper
Plain lining paper is designed to cover poor wall surfaces before they are papered (or painted), and can significantly improve the end result of your decorating. Sold in five thicknesses, heavier and thicker paper is less likely to tear. The rolls are often twice the length of a roll of ordinary wallpaper, so check the length on the roll and work out how many rolls you will need. You will buy too much if you assume that you need the same number of rolls as the wallpaper you choose.
Paste Use cold-water or all-purpose.

LINING PAPER
If you are going to paper a room after lining it, make sure that the seams in the two papers won't fall in the same place.
• Start with a half-width of lining paper to stagger the joints.
• Do not overlap the edges: raised areas will show through.
• Do not take lining paper around corners. Trim away any excess paper so that the edges fit neatly.

Woodchip Useful for covering uneven walls, this paper has two layers bonded together with a sprinkling of wood chippings between them. Paint with emulsion. Rough to the touch, so not suitable in children's rooms or in narrow passages.
Paste Use all-purpose, cold-water, heavy-duty or ready mixed.

Standard wallpaper Quality varies with price: cheap paper is thin and tears easily, especially when damp. It is also more difficult to hang. None of these papers is washable, so avoid using them in kitchens.
Paste Use all-purpose, cold-water or ready-mixed.

Tips on buying wallpaper

Count the widths Use a standard 530mm-wide wallpaper roll as a measuring stick to estimate how many strips will be needed to paper all the way round a room. Count doors and average-size windows as wall – the extra paper will be used up in trimming and pattern matching – but ignore large windows and patio doors.
Multiply the metric height of the room by the number of strips to get the total length of paper required. Divide this figure by the length of a standard roll (10m) to find out how many rolls you'll need.

Remember the repeat If your chosen paper has a random pattern – a sponging effect for example – or if it is plain stripes, you will need fewer rolls of paper than if there is a pattern with a drop between the repeats. Pattern repeats can vary from around 75mm to 500mm or more. The pattern repeat length is generally noted on the wallpaper wrapper.

   If the paper you have chosen has a large repeat, you will probably get one fewer full length out of each roll than you think, so always buy an extra roll or two. Some stores will allow you to return unused rolls if they are left unopened and you have retained your receipt.

Keep to one batch Check that all the paper comes from the same batch, to avoid colour variation between rolls. If you have to buy rolls with a different batch number, because the store does not have enough from the same batch, aim to use them in areas where any slight shading variations will not show, such as behind furniture or tucked away in a poorly lit corner.

Best for beginners For your first attempt at paperhanging, choose a paper with no pattern match (or with a random pattern) so you have one less thing to worry about as you hang each length.

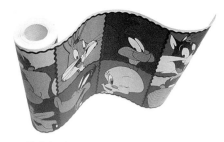

Quick change Borders can be used on painted or papered walls. Some are self-adhesive; others need pasting. Use ready-mixed border adhesive for applying a border over a washable or vinyl wall covering. Ordinary powder wallpaper paste will not stick to them.

How to hang wallpaper

You can achieve a gratifying and rapid transformation with wallpaper, and the job is less daunting than you might think. The first stage is measuring and marking out.

1 First, mark a vertical guide on the wall. Start in a corner and measure out to the width of a roll of paper minus 25mm, to allow a strip of paper to turn onto the adjacent wall. Make a pencil mark.
Pin the top of a plumb line to the wall at ceiling level, so it hangs down over the mark. Make pencil marks down the wall immediately behind the line and join them up with a ruler. Make sure that the line is never more than your original measurement away from the corner (because the corner is not true). If this happens, draw another plumb line closer to the corner. Always draw a new line when you start papering the next wall.

2 Take a roll of paper and check which way the pattern goes. With a steel tape, measure the wall height down to the top of the skirting board. Add an extra 100mm for trimming at the top and bottom.

3 Unroll the paper on the pasting table, pattern-side down, measure the length and draw a line with a pencil and straightedge across the back.

4 Cut along the line with a pair of long-bladed wallpapering scissors.

5 Turn the paper over, unroll the next length and match the pattern by placing it edge-to-edge with the first length. Using the cut as a measuring guide, cut off the second length.
   Continue in this way until several lengths are ready for pasting. Number them on the back so that you know the hanging order and note which end is the top.

Pasting the paper

1 Lay the cut lengths on the pasting table, pattern side down.

2 Position the top piece of paper so that all the spare paper hangs off the table to the right. If you are left-handed, reverse all the following paper-hanging procedures.

3 Adjust the paper so that the long edge aligns with the edge of the table.

4 Load the paste brush and wipe off excess paste by dragging the brush across the string on the bucket.

5 Brush the paste down the centre of the paper, then out to the edges. If any paste gets onto the table, wipe it off with a damp cloth.

6 Check that all the paper is evenly covered with paste, especially the edges. Holding the left-hand edge, loosely fold the paper over – paste side to paste side – to about the centre of the length.

7 Slide the paper to the left of the table so that the pasted part hangs off the edge.

8 Paste the right-hand end of the paper as you did the left, brushing in a herringbone pattern until the paper is all pasted.

9 Fold the paper over – without creasing it – so the top and bottom edges meet.

10 Leave the pasted paper to soak for as long as the manufacturer recommends. Thin paper and vinyl will be ready to hang almost immediately but heavier materials need to be left for 10 to 15 minutes.

HELPFUL TIPS

Guarantee a clean cut
A build-up of paste on the blades stops wallpaper scissors from cutting cleanly. Keep a bowl of water nearby and get into the habit of dipping the blades into it every time you trim the waste from a length of pasted paper. Dry the scissors before using them again.

Hanging the paper

1 Carry the pasted length to the wall and release the top fold gently. Do not let the lower half suddenly drop – it may tear, or stretch and cause matching problems.

2 Hold the top right corner against the wall so that the right-hand edge of the paper aligns with the pencil line. Make sure about 50mm of excess paper is left at the top of the wall for trimming.

3 Keep the left edge of the paper off the wall while you continue to align the right-hand edge down the pencil line.

4 Once the right edge is in place, smooth the paper with your hand or paperhanging brush diagonally up until the top left corner of the paper is on the wall.

5 Smooth out the top half of the length with the paper-hanging brush, working from the centre outwards. Make sure the paper stays on the pencil line.

6 Now release the lower fold. Brush down the centre of the length, then out to the edges as you did when pasting, ensuring that any bubbles are brushed out. Dab down the edges with the tip of the brush or a dry, clean cloth made into a pad.

7 With the length in place, run the back of a pair of scissors along the paper where it meets the skirting board, to crease it.

8 Pull the paper gently away from the wall and cut along the crease, with the underside of the paper facing you. Brush the trimmed edge back in place. Repeat this process at the top of the length.

Hanging the next lengths

1 Hang the second length of paper to the right of the piece on the wall, following the same procedure but without using the plumb line. Match the top section of the left edge of the new length with the length on the wall, then run your hand diagonally up and to the right to press the top of the paper to the wall.

2 Smooth out the paper from the centre with the paperhanging brush.

3 Release the lower fold, check that the edges match and continue to brush over the paper. Trim top and bottom as before.

4 With two or three pieces hung, you can run a seam roller lightly down the joins of smooth papers. Do not press down the edges of textured materials, like Anaglypta, or lines will show where the pattern has been flattened.

Tackling the tricky bits

Switches and sockets Hang wallpaper straight over a light switch or wall socket so that the fitting marks the surface of the paper. Pierce the paper over the centre of the fitting and make diagonal cuts out to the four corners. With the power off, unscrew the faceplate and pull it away from the wall. Then trim off all but about 15mm of the paper triangles and trap the rest behind the faceplate.

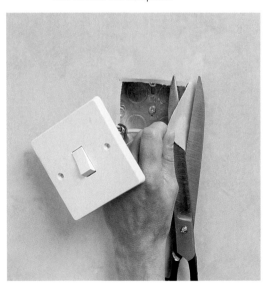

AVOID TROUBLE WITH BUBBLES

Allow paste to soak in Before pasting wallpaper, read the hanging instructions to see how much time you should allow for the paste to soak in. Wallpaper expands when it gets wet, and if you hang a length while this expansion is still going on, the paper will form bubbles as it stretches and lifts away from the wall surface. The thicker and heavier the paper is, the more time will be needed for this expansion to stop – as much as 15 minutes in the case of some heavy embossed papers. Each length you paste should be left to soak for precisely the same time.

New paper over old Don't risk trying to paper over existing wallpaper. The new paste will soak into the old paper, softening its paste, and both layers will then bubble up on the wall. Always strip old paper first.

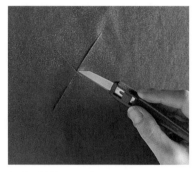

An invisible repair A bubble that doesn't flatten out as the paste dries is usually caused by careless pasting leaving a dry spot on the back of the paper. Make two cuts across the bubble at 90° with a sharp trimming knife (above) or razor blade. Peel back the flaps and apply a little paste with a small paintbrush, then press the flaps back into place with your paperhanging brush.

Wash off grease spots Greasy marks on the walls will cause bubbles because the wallpaper can't stick properly. Wash the surfaces down thoroughly with household detergent or sugar soap before you start papering.

Turning an internal corner Don't try to hang a full-width strip of wallpaper round an internal corner. The corner will probably not be truly square, so the edge of the turned section of paper won't be vertical and that will misalign every length on the next wall.

Measure the distance from the edge of the last full length to the corner, and cut a length of paper to that dimension, plus about 15mm for turning around the corner onto the next wall.

Measure the width of the remainder of the cut length and mark a plumb line this distance from the corner on the next wall. Hang the length to this line so its other edge overlaps the turned strip (above).

Turning an external corner Use a technique similar to that for internal corners. Cut the strip of paper that reaches the corner so that about 25mm will turn onto the next wall, and hang it. Then hang the offcut on the next wall. You'll be able to butt it to the turned edge if the corner is true. If it is not, hang it to a plumbed line so it just overlaps the turned edge, then cut through both layers, using a straightedge and a very sharp trimming knife (above). Peel away the offcuts and finish the two edges with a seam roller.

Masking a crease Wallpaper may crease as you turn it round an out-of-square corner. If it does, tear the paper along the crease line while it's still wet, then smooth it back into place with the 'white' of the tear on the underside. The repair will be almost invisible.

Don't tear vinyl: cut the crease instead and use vinyl overlap adhesive to stick the cut edges down.

Special treatment for vinyls Vinyl will not stick over vinyl, so when you overlap edges at a corner, either cut through both thicknesses to make a butt joint or stick the two together with vinyl overlap adhesive.

Papering behind radiators If you are unable to remove the radiators before papering a room, cut the paper to length so you can tuck about 200mm down behind them. Use a radiator paint roller if you have one to press the paper into place. Otherwise improvise by taping some sponge to a slim batten.

Invisible patches If you have to patch badly marked or damaged wallpaper, tear rather than cut the patch so the 'feathered' edges will blend in with the surrounding paper. Then stick the patch over the damage with a little wallpaper paste.

To repair vinyl wallpaper, cut the patch. Hold an offcut over the damaged area, align the pattern and cut through both layers with a sharp trimming knife (below). Peel off the vinyl top layer, remove the backing paper with a wallpaper scraper, then align the patch and stick it on.

Revamping old tiles

You may have inherited tired and dated old tiles in your new bathroom or kitchen. Removing old tiles and retiling is a major undertaking; in the meantime, here are some ideas to improve what you've already got.

Grout is the filling compound used in the gaps between ceramic tiles. It is normally white, although coloured grouting is also available, and often discolours over time. A wall of dull tiles can be given an instant lift by cleaning, replacing, or even painting the old grout.

Mould on grout Dark stains on grout lines may be caused by mould, which thrives in damp and warmth. Do not use bleach. It will not destroy the roots of the mould. Instead, kill the mould with a proprietary fungicide, following the manufacturer's instructions. Any stains left on the grout can be hidden by painting on grout whitener. When the whitener is dry, apply more fungicide to prevent further mould.

Clean between the tiles A toothbrush is the ideal tool for cleaning grout. Remove dirt and grease with a solution of liquid detergent in warm water or a non-abrasive cream cleaner. Don't use abrasive cleaners on tiled surfaces; they may dull the glaze and 'pit' the grout.

Replace missing grout If there are gaps in the grout, rake out all old grout with a proprietary grout rake, a small-toothed tool designed for the job. Draw the rake along the grout lines, first vertically and then horizontally, to remove the old grout to a depth of about 3mm.

Use a small, stiff-bristled brush to remove all the debris from the joints before regrouting. If you've never grouted tiles, a small piece of natural sponge is the best tool to start with. Once you've gained confidence, however, a rubber squeegee (above) does a quicker job, followed by a wipe with the sponge.

Finishing touch A ball-point pen cap makes an excellent tool for recessing narrow grouting joints. A lollipop stick will also do the trick. Work while the grout is soft, carefully wiping away the surplus with a damp sponge. Don't be tempted to use your fingertip, though; grout is surprisingly abrasive and will soon rub your skin raw.

Bring back the sparkle A solution of borax or liquid household ammonia in hot water will revive tiled surfaces discoloured by dirt and grease. Rinse the tiles with clean water then dry them off with a chamois leather. **Remove soap splashes** with a mix of 1 part white vinegar to 4 parts water. Rinse with clean water and then wipe it dry.

Crazed tiles Tiles may become crazed because they are old, but new tiles may also be affected if water gets behind them. Nothing can be done to repair tiles damaged by crazing. You can paint tiles with special tile paint, though this is not as

TILES

tough a finish as the original glaze. If you have or can buy spare matching tiles, you can remove the damaged ones and replace them (see below).

Replace old sealant In the corner of a shower cubicle, or where kitchen tiles meet the worktop, for example, the sealant may be stained and lifting away. Rake out the old sealant and run a bead of new waterproof sealant along the join. Use sealant rather than grout at joins in corners to accommodate any slight movement.

Replacing a damaged tile

If you work carefully, it is a fairly straightforward task to replace a single cracked tile or remove and replace one with holes drilled in it that are no longer needed.

Tools *Power drill; large masonry bit; cold chisel; hammer; safety goggles; work gloves; grouting tools.*

Materials *New tile; tile adhesive with integral notched spreader; grout.*

Before you start Protect your hands with sturdy gloves, and wear safety goggles to shield your eyes from slivers of glaze that will splinter from the tile as you work.

1 Drill holes in the centre of the tile you want to remove, using a power drill and masonry bit.

2 Insert the cold chisel, and hammer from the holes outwards towards the edges to get behind the tile.

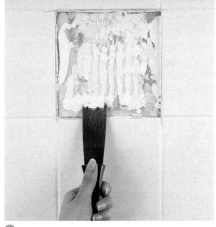

3 When you have removed the tile, carefully chisel out the old adhesive until you reveal bare wall.

4 Butter the back of a new tile with adhesive, using the notched spreader, and fit it in place. Put spacers around the tile to ensure even spacing.

5 Lay a straightedge or offcut of timber across the repair to check that the wall is flat, adding or removing adhesive as necessary.

6 Use a damp cloth to wipe excess adhesive from the surface of the tiles. Leave the adhesive to set for about 12 hours before grouting the joins.

Choosing floor coverings

There are many types of floor covering, with new materials being introduced all the time. Replacing an old carpet with a new laminate wood floor, or stripping old floorboards, can give a room a terrific lift. Here is a summary of what is available.

Sanded and varnished floorboards

• Suitable finish for boards in good condition and without gaps.
• The floor is sanded with a heavy-duty sanding machine that can be hired for a day or weekend. Cheap, and fairly simple to do yourself (see page 84). Sanding a floor is noisy and dusty work, however.
• The finished surface is noisy underfoot. Can be draughty on a ground floor if boards are not tongued-and-grooved.
• Sweep or vacuum-clean frequently to remove grit, which can scratch the surface.

Wipe up spillages with a damp cloth. Polish regularly. Lightly sand worn areas and re-varnish.

Vinyl tiles
• Huge range of colours, patterns and price. Available in imitation ceramic, wood or stone as well as cheaper smooth vinyl.
• Hygienic, easily cleaned. Resistant to spillages. Good for kitchens and bathrooms.
• Smooth vinyl tiles are slippery when wet. Cushion-backed versions are warmer, safer and quieter underfoot.
• Clean as for sheet vinyl (right), but beware of using too much water; water could get under the joins.

Cork tiles
• Natural material, available in various finishes. Warmer material than vinyl.
• Easily cleaned when varnished or bought factory sealed. PVC-coated cork is best.
• Can become worn in heavy traffic areas unless the tiles are PVC-coated.
• Vacuum-clean or sweep regularly to remove surface dirt, and wash with solution of mild detergent. Avoid swamping with water, and do not use abrasive cleaners.

Ceramic tiles
• Range from traditional square or rectangular tiles to specialist, handmade tiles of various shapes. Some ceramic tiles are very slippery, but tiles can be obtained with an anti-slip surface.
• Long lasting, easily cleaned and highly resistant to stains and spillages. Wide choice of patterns and colours.
• Unglazed ceramic tiles tend to be porous, and are not suitable for kitchens and bathrooms.
• Expensive. Timber sub-floor needs strengthening before laying. Noisy underfoot. Cold if walked on in bare feet. Crockery breaks if dropped on it.
• Remove surface grit by sweeping or vacuum cleaning, then wash with non-abrasive detergent in water. Keep water to a minimum to prevent seepage under tiles.

FINISHES FOR STRIPPED FLOORBOARDS

• Special hardwearing floor paints are available, or you can simply use emulsion and then coat it with a flooring-grade varnish. Brighten up the floor with stencils before varnishing, or paint alternate boards in carnival stripes.
• You can give a floor an attractive 'limewashed' finish with slightly diluted emulsion paint, and apply clear varnish over it once the paint is dry.
• Buy a wax-based liming paste, which you rub into the bare wood with a coarse cloth and then wipe off. However, you can't apply varnish over wax (it will not bond or dry properly), so you will have to finish the floor with clear wax polish. This is hard work to apply and maintain, and not very durable.

Terracotta and quarry tiles

• Terracotta tiles and their budget-priced alternative, quarry tiles, are a more rustic alternative to ceramic tiles. Quarry tiles are less porous than terracotta tiles, but do not have the subtle shading of terracotta.

• Terracotta is warmer underfoot than other hard floor tiles. Both types are hard-wearing and can be cleaned easily. Good choice of brown and red shades.

• Noisy when walked on and not kind to dropped crockery. Their thickness makes them difficult to cut. If laid on a timber floor, these tiles require a 13mm plywood underlay.

• Terracotta tiles need a primer or treatment applied before installation, plus a regular wax or seal to maintain their surface finish.

Sheet vinyl

• Smooth vinyl is cheaper; cushioned vinyl is softer underfoot. Wide range of patterns and colours. Linoleum is a traditional floor covering that has recently regained popularity. It can be more difficult to lay but is very durable and more resistant to burns than vinyl. It comes in a range of colours and patterns.

• Hygienic, easily cleaned, resistant to spillages. Inexpensive flooring for kitchens and bathrooms.

• Smooth vinyl is slippery when wet. Cushion-backed varieties are warmer, safer and quieter underfoot.

• Vacuum-clean or sweep to remove grit, which can scratch. Wash with detergent. Remove scuff marks by gently rubbing with fine steel wool lubricated with white spirit, taking care not to rub through top surface.

Carpet

• Wide range of colour and price. Available as fitted carpet, carpet squares or carpet tiles. Gives feeling of warmth and comfort. Graded according to use – from heavily used stairs to low-use spare bedrooms.

• Good quality carpet is expensive. Spillages may cause permanent staining.

• Vacuum-clean frequently to remove grit which can harm fibres. Remove stains with proprietary cleaner. Rearrange carpet tiles to even out wear.

Wood and laminate

• Wood floors come as strips or mosaic panels. Some are nailed down, some are stuck down, and some simply interlock and 'float' on the floor below. Because solid timber is so expensive, most wood floors are laminate floors, consisting of a thin top veneer layer fixed to a strong bottom layer of softwood or high density fibreboard (HDF). There are many inexpensive DIY versions available.

• Natural wood is luxurious and long-lasting in living rooms, dining rooms and halls.

• Natural wood is expensive. Laminated wood strip is cheaper, but the cheapest printed types do not wear well. Noisy underfoot.

• Remove surface dirt with vacuum cleaner to minimise scratching. Varnished floors can be wiped with a damp cloth.

Natural fibres

• Coir, jute, seagrass and sisal flooring are all made from plant fibres: coir from coconut husks; jute from the plant of the same name; seagrass from grasses grown in paddy fields; and sisal from the fleshy-leaved plant Agave sisalana.

• They come in a variety of weaves. A latex backing means the plant-fibre floor covering will not fray when cut to size, and can be laid with or without underlay.

• Durability differs: coir and sisal floor coverings tend to be more durable, seagrass and jute less so.

• They can stain and are vulnerable to damp – therefore they are not suitable for kitchens and bathrooms. Some are not suitable for use on stairs: the finish can be slippery or not hard-wearing enough.

• Vacuum-clean on a regular basis to ensure removal of grit that can harm fibres. Some types can be shampooed; others must be dry-cleaned.

Restoring a wood floor

An attractive floor can be created by restoring existing floorboards. Floorboards may be stripped and varnished, or you could stain, paint or lime them before sealing with a hardwearing clear coating.

Filling holes in floorboards

Use a flexible filler to cover all nail and screw heads – nail heads should be punched below the surface, and screws may need countersinking so that their heads are below the surface. If you are painting the floor, the filler colour does not matter; if you are varnishing it, choose a filler slightly lighter in colour than the surrounding floor. Once dry, sand filler flush with the floor.

Plugging gaps between boards

Fill narrow gaps with flexible mastic (clear mastic will be almost invisible); wider gaps are best filled with thin lengths of square-edge moulding.

1 Plane moulding strips into a slight wedge shape.

2 Apply a little woodworking adhesive before tapping a wedge into a gap, thin edge first.

3 Plane wedges down to floor level when the adhesive has set, then stain them to match the boards.

Sanding a wood floor

Sanding a floor is hard, dusty, noisy work. On fairly new boards that have not been stained or become too dirty, sanding may not be necessary. Get rid of surface dirt by scrubbing with detergent and hot water.

Tools Dust mask; nail punch and claw hammer; floor sanding machine and edging sander (a weekend's hire should be enough for one room); earmuffs; sanding belts and discs (coarse, medium and fine); paint roller and wide paintbrush; fine steel wool.

Materials Flooring-grade varnish or other finish.

Before you start Remove furnishings and fixtures. Sanding floorboards creates a great deal of fine dust, despite the collection bag on the machine, so take down curtains, lampshades, pictures and other removable wall and ceiling fixtures. Polythene sheets pinned over door frames will help to keep the rest of the house dust free.

1 Punch in all the nails in the floor, otherwise they will tear the sanding belts. Clean off traces of old polish with steel wool dipped in white spirit; otherwise the polish will clog up the sanding belt.

WARNING

Empty the dust bag as soon as it is about one-third full. Bulked wood dust can ignite spontaneously, especially if it is impregnated with old stain or varnish. Also empty the bag whenever you stop work for more than a few minutes.

2 Wearing protective gloves, start at the edge of the room with your back against the wall. Keep the sander slightly away from the skirting board at the side otherwise you may damage it.

3 Work along the length of the boards, as sanding across them causes scratches. But if the boards curl up at the edges, make the first runs diagonally across them with a coarse belt. Finish with medium and fine belts along the length of the boards.

HELPFUL TIP

When using a floor sander, adopt a start and stop routine. Press down on the handle or operate a special lever to raise the drum off the boards before starting or stopping. If you allow the drum to be in contact with the boards while building up to full speed or slowing down, they will be scarred.

---

4 On a floor where not very much stripping is needed, let the machine go forwards at a slow steady pace to the far end of the room, lifting up the drum as soon as you reach the skirting board.

5 If the boards are badly marked, wheel the sander backwards to your start point, lower the drum and make a second pass over the first one.
Never pull the sander backwards when the drum is rotating, or the machine may pull sideways out of control and score the floor surface badly.

6 When the strip looks clean, move on to the next one, and continue to the end of the room. Raise the belt as you change direction, or it may damage the boards. You will have started each run about a metre out from the wall behind you. When you have covered the room, turn the machine round, and deal with that area.

Sanding the edges

Once you are left with a narrow border all round the room that the sander cannot reach, move on to an edging sander (a disc on a power drill is not powerful enough).

1 Use the edging sander all round the edges of the room, taking care not to damage the paint on the skirting boards.

2 Vacuum-clean the floor to get rid of all the wood dust. Do not damp the floor as the water may leave marks.

3 Finally, wipe the floor with a clean, dry, lint-free cloth. Be sure to shake it frequently outdoors to get rid of the dust particles.

Finishing the floor

Buy a new brush Don't risk getting specks of old paint or bristles in the varnish by using an old or cheap brush. Invest in a new, good-quality brush before you start. Synthetic fibre brushes are less prone to hair loss than natural bristle types.
　　Use a narrow brush to varnish the edge trims and the perimeter boards, then switch to a wider brush for fast coverage of the rest of the floor.

Alternative to varnish An oil polish will provide a hard-wearing alternative to varnish, and is well worth the effort if you have a beautiful old timber floor. Use a product such as Danish oil, or mix your own using 1 part of raw linseed oil to 8 parts of turpentine.
　　Warm the oil to make it more fluid and to help absorption. It could be 24 hours or more before the floor is dry enough for a second, more sparing coat. Keep applying coats until buffing raises a silky sheen, and water forms beads on the surface.

Electrics

Electrical emergencies

WARNING: the main on-off switch on your consumer unit disconnects only the fuses or miniature circuit breakers (MCBs) and the cables leading out from it to the household circuits. It does NOT disconnect the cables entering via the meter from the service cable. Do not tamper with these cables. They are always live at mains voltage.

Fire in an appliance

1 If a plug-in appliance catches fire, switch the appliance off at the socket outlet and pull out the plug.

2 If a fixed appliance with no plug is on fire, turn it off at the wall switch if you can, or at the main switch on the consumer unit (see below).

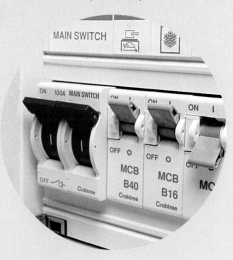

3 Do not use water on an electrical fire. Smother the fire with a rug or blanket, or use a dry-powder fire extinguisher.

4 Get the appliance checked (and repaired if necessary) by an expert before you use it again. Otherwise, replace it.

Smell of overheating

1 If you smell burning from an appliance, turn off the switch at the socket and pull out the plug. If it is a fixed appliance with no plug, turn off its wall switch or the main switch at the consumer unit. Turn off the appliance switch and call an expert. An electrician can check flex connections, renew them if necessary and, if they are sound, check the appliance. If the appliance is under guarantee, call the supplier.

2 If the smell comes from a socket outlet or a plug, turn off the main switch at the consumer unit. If the plug is hot, let it cool before unplugging it. Then check its connections, including the fuse contacts, and examine the flex for damage. Replace the plug if necessary (page 96). If the socket is hot, call an electrician.

No electricity

1 If power throughout your house fails and neighbouring houses are also without power, there is a mains supply failure. Report it to the 24-hour emergency number under 'Electricity' in the phone book.

2 If your system is protected by a whole-house residual current device (RCD), check whether it has switched itself off. Try to switch it on again if it has.

3 If it will not switch on, the fault that tripped it off is still present on the system. **Call an electrician to track it down and rectify it.**

4 If you do not have an RCD and your house is the only one without power, there may be a fault in your supply cable or your main supply fuse may have blown. Do not touch it. Report the power failure as above.

Minor emergencies

1 If one appliance fails to work, unplug it and check its plug, fuse and flex; renew them as necessary. If the appliance still fails to work, plug it in a different socket outlet to test it. If it works, the problem is with the original socket; if not, take the appliance to an expert for repair.

2 If all lights or appliances on one circuit stop working, switch off at the consumer unit and check the circuit fuse (page 94). If it is sound, there may be a fault in the circuit cable. **Call in an electrician to track it down and rectify it.**

Electric shock

WARNING: If you get a minor shock from an electrical appliance, a plug or other wiring accessory, stop using it immediately.

• Get a repair expert to check the appliance for earth safety, and replace damaged plugs and wiring accessories as soon as possible. Use PVC insulating tape to make a temporary repair.

• If someone receives a major shock, DO NOT touch bare flesh while the person is in contact with the source of the current. If you do, the current will pass through you as well, giving you an electric shock.

1 Immediately turn off the source of the current if you can.

2 If you cannot do this, grab the person's clothing and drag them away from the source of the current, or stand on some insulating material such as a book, and use a broom or a similar wooden object to move the person or the current source.

3 Lay a conscious but visibly shocked person flat on their back with their legs raised slightly and cover with a blanket. Do not give food, drink or cigarettes. Cool visible burns with cold water, then cover with a dry sterile dressing. Do not apply ointments. Call an ambulance.

If someone is unconscious Place an unconscious person in the recovery position (above). Tilt the head back and bring the jaw forward to keep the airway clear. Cover them with a blanket and call an ambulance.

Check the person's breathing Monitor breathing and heartbeat continuously until the ambulance arrives. If either stops, give artificial ventilation or external chest compression, if you are trained to do so.

The electrical system

Before you do any electrical work you should get to grips with the different types of circuit in your home.

Electric power is measured in **watts** (W). The flow of electricity is called current, and is measured in **amps** (A). The driving force, or pressure, of the current is measured in **volts** (V). The pressure of public supply in Britain has been standardised at 230 volts. In Britain, mains electricity is **alternating current** (AC) and the electricity from batteries is **direct current** (DC). The advantage of alternating current is that it can be transformed from one voltage to another so a power station can supply a very high voltage to substations that reduce the voltage to 230V to supply homes.

Lighting circuit The circuit runs out from the consumer unit, linking a chain of lighting points. A cable runs from each lighting point to its switch. The circuit is protected by a 5 or 6amp circuit fuse or MCB. It can safely supply up to a maximum of about 1200 watts, but in practice should not serve more than ten lighting points. The circuit would be overloaded if each of the lighting points had high-wattage bulbs.

Ring main circuit The circuit is wired as a ring that starts from the consumer unit and returns to it, allowing current to flow to socket outlets either way round the ring. It can serve a floor area of up to 100m². It is protected by a 30 or 32amp circuit fuse or MCB. It can have any number of sockets or fused connection units on it, but its maximum total load is about 7000 watts. For larger total loads and larger floor areas, additional ring circuits are needed.

Spur on a ring circuit Extra socket outlets can be added to an existing ring main circuit via spurs branching off the ring at a socket outlet or junction box. In theory, each outlet on the ring could supply a spur to a single or double socket or a fused connection unit. However, the circuit including any spurs must not serve rooms with a floor area of more than 100m² – and its maximum load is still 7000 watts.

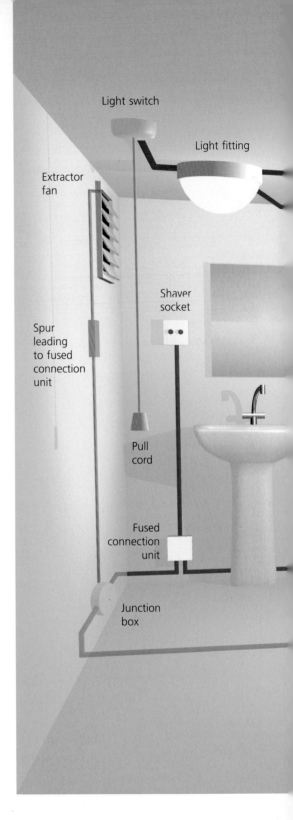

Light switch

Light fitting

Extractor fan

Shaver socket

Spur leading to fused connection unit

Pull cord

Fused connection unit

Junction box

Socket outlet The maximum load that can be supplied by a socket outlet taking a 13amp plug is 3000 watts. The plug is fitted with a 13amp or a 3amp fuse, according to the wattage rating of the appliance connected to it.

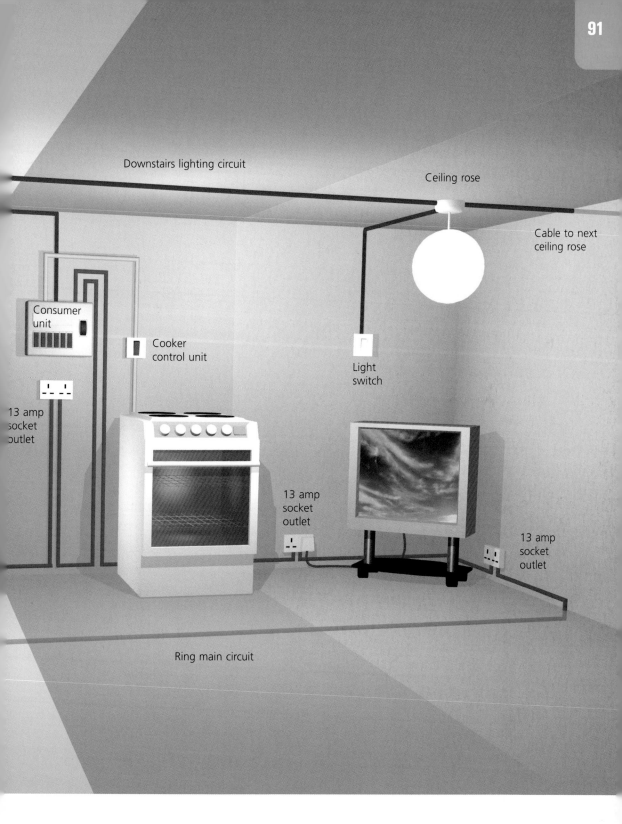

Downstairs lighting circuit

Ceiling rose

Cable to next
ceiling rose

Consumer
unit

Cooker
control unit

Light
switch

13 amp
socket
outlet

13 amp
socket
outlet

13 amp
socket
outlet

Ring main circuit

Single-appliance circuit An appliance that is a large
consumer of electricity and in constant or frequent use –
a cooker, a fixed water heater, or a shower heater unit, for
example – has its own circuit running from the consumer unit.
It would take too large a proportion of the power available on
a shared circuit and would be likely to cause an overload.

The consumer unit

Modern fuse boards – called consumer units – may look different from home to home, but the basic components are the same.

Consumer unit The householder's responsibility for the system begins here. It houses the main on-off switch, the earthing terminal block for all the house circuits, and individual fuses or miniature circuit breakers (MCBs) for each one.

• The number of circuits varies according to a household's needs, but always includes separate lighting and power circuits.
• **Label the MCBs** to show which circuit each one protects. To identify the circuits, switch off one MCB at a time and check which lights or appliances are not working.

Service cable Electricity enters the home through the service (supply) cable – usually buried underground in urban areas, but often run overhead in rural areas. It carries electricity at 230 volts. The current flows along the live conductor and returns along the neutral conductor. Never interfere with the service cable, which is the property of your electricity supply company. The term 'live' has been replaced by 'line' or 'phase' in the electrical industry. Live and neutral imply that current flows only in the live conductor, whereas both carry current at all times. The terms live and neutral are used throughout this book as they are familiar.

Miniature circuit breakers (MCBs) Modern consumer units have MCBs instead of fuses. If too much current is demanded, the circuit is disconnected instantly and a switch moves to the 'off' position or a button pops out. Reset the switch to restore power to the circuit.

MCB CURRENT RATINGS

European standardisation means the ratings of new MCBs are being changed:
  5amp becomes 6amp
  15amp becomes 16amp
  30amp becomes 32amp
  45amp becomes 40amp.

Sealed unit/service cut-out The service cable ends here. It is a deliberate 'weak link' that will melt if more current is demanded than the service cable can safely supply, disconnecting supply to the house. **Do not tamper with the sealed unit.**

Circuit cables Individual circuits are supplied by cables running out from the consumer unit.
• The live conductor in each circuit cable is connected to a terminal on its fuse or MCB.
• The neutral conductor connects to the main neutral terminal block in the consumer unit.
• The earth conductor connects to the main earthing terminal block.

WIRING REGULATIONS

Since January 2005, all new domestic wiring work in England and Wales must comply with the requirements of a new section of the Building Regulations. Part P, entitled Electrical Safety, covers the design, installation, inspection and testing of electrical work in the home. It applies to both professional and DIY electrical work.

What you need to know:

1 You can still do your own wiring work, but it must be inspected, tested and certified by a professional electrician.

2 Any minor work that is not on a fixed electrical installation (for example, lamps and other appliances that can be unplugged) does not need approval.

3 You must notify your local authority building control department before you start major wiring jobs and pay a fee for inspection and testing when the job is completed.

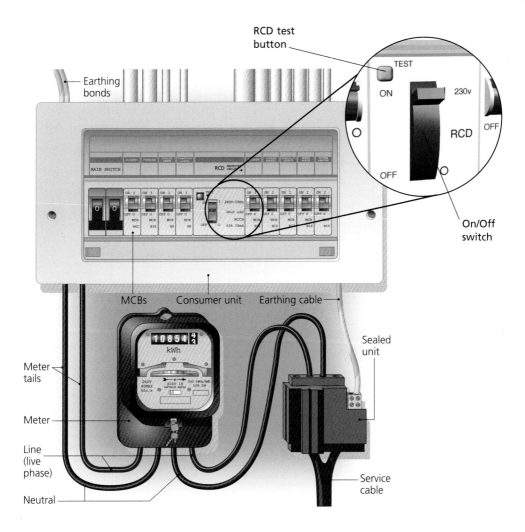

RCD test button

Earthing bonds

TEST
ON   230v
RCD   OFF
OFF

On/Off switch

MAIN SWITCH   RCD

MCBs   Consumer unit   Earthing cable

Sealed unit

Meter tails

Meter

Line (live phase)

Neutral

Service cable

Time to upgrade If your new home has an old-fashioned fuse box, consider getting it replaced with a modern consumer unit containing miniature circuit breakers (MCBs) (above). This is a relatively costly job, but it will make your electrics much safer and more convenient, as well as adding value to your home.

Residual current device (RCD) An RCD monitors the balance of the live and neutral current flows. An imbalance occurs if current leaks from a circuit because of faulty insulation, or because someone has touched a live part and received an electric shock. If the RCD detects an imbalance, it switches off the supply immediately – fast enough to prevent an electric shock from being fatal.
• An RCD is installed to protect only at-risk circuits such as those to socket outlets and some stand-alone appliances.
• An RCD in its own enclosure may have been added to an existing installation to protect new at-risk circuits.

Meter A two-tariff meter with dual displays may be installed to allow the use of night-rate electricity for storage heaters.

Earthing cable This connects the earthing terminal block in the consumer unit (to which all the circuit cables are connected) to the earthing point provided by the electricity supply company – usually on the service cut-out or the service cable. Earth cross-bonding cables connect metal gas and water supply pipework to the earthing terminal block.

Meter tails These two cables (live and neutral) link the sealed unit to the meter and the meter to the consumer unit.
• The live cable is covered with red insulation and the neutral cable with black.
• Each tail has an outer sheath which may either be grey or match the colour of the insulation sheath.
• The electricity supply company must disconnect the supply before any work can be carried out on the meter tails.

Does your wiring need replacing?

If your home has an old wiring system, it may be unsafe. Your survey may have alerted you to the problem, but check for these tell-tale signs. Rewiring is the only solution – a job for a qualified electrician.

Check the main fuse board
Look for cables from the meter going to a metal box with a main on/off switch for the installation. There may be separate switched fuse boxes for each circuit. Inside the fuse boxes there may be circuit fuses in porcelain holders. Such a system is old, likely to be unsafe, and should be replaced.

Old light switches
Round brass or Bakelite light switches mounted on wooden blocks are signs of a lighting system that is over 50 years old. The lighting circuits should be rewired with new cable and fittings as soon as possible.

Old wiring – new fittings
You may have a system where the old rubber-insulated cables remain, but the switches and sockets have been replaced by modern ones. Look at the circuit cables where they emerge from the fuse box. If you find old cables, have them checked by an electrician, and plan to have the system rewired as soon as possible.

Round-pin sockets
If you have old-style round-pin sockets, your wiring system is likely to be 50 or more years old. It should be completely rewired without delay for safety reasons.

Mending a fuse

If you still have circuit fuses (below), keep spare fuses or fuse wire to hand for instant repairs if a fuse 'blows'.

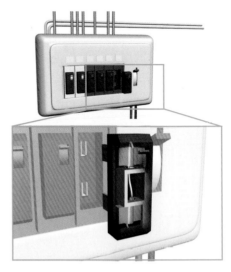

Replacing fuse wire

1 Turn off the main on/off switch on the consumer unit. Remove or open the cover over the fuse carriers.

2 Pull out each fuse carrier (see opposite for types of carrier) in turn to find out which has blown. Scorch marks often show this, or a break in the wire.

3 If a power circuit is affected, switch off and unplug all the appliances on the circuit. If it is a lighting circuit, turn off all the light switches. If you do not switch everything off, the mended fuse is likely to blow again immediately you turn the mains back on.

4 Loosen the two terminal screws and remove any pieces of old wire. Cut a new piece of fuse wire of the correct amp rating, long enough to cross the carrier and go round both screws.

5 Wind the wire clockwise round one screw and tighten the screw. Pass the wire across the bridge or thread it through the holder. If you are unsure about how the wire runs in the carrier, examine one of the intact fuses.

6 Wind the wire clockwise round the second screw. Make sure there is a little slack in the wire so that it will not snap and then tighten the screw.

TYPES OF REWIRABLE FUSE CARRIER

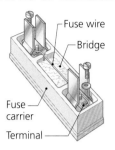

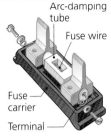

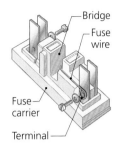

Bridged fuse The wire runs from one terminal to the other over a plug of white arc-damping material. The carrier is ceramic.

Protected fuse Between the terminals the wire runs through a porcelain arc-damping tube. The carrier is tough plastic.

Fuse between humps The unprotected wire passes round humps between one terminal and the other. The carrier is ceramic.

7 Replace the fuse carrier in the consumer unit. Close the cover and restore the power by turning on the main switch. Then check the circuit (see right)

Replacing a cartridge fuse

1 Turn off the main switch on the consumer unit. If you have cartridge fuses, you will need a fuse tester that will tell you if a cartridge fuse has blown.

2 Find out which fuse has blown: take out each fuse carrier in turn so you can test the cartridge.

3 Prise the cartridge gently from the clamps. Some carriers are in two halves and the screw holding them together has to be removed to give access to the cartridge.

4 Remove one carrier at a time; test its cartridge with a fuse tester, and replace it before removing the next one for testing. When you have traced the blown fuse, replace the cartridge with a new one of the amp rating shown on the carrier.

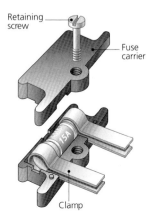

5 As with a rewirable fuse, switch off all appliances or lights on the affected circuit. Replace the fuse carrier, close the box and turn on the main switch. Then check the circuit.

Checking the circuit

Look for damage on the appliances, lights and flexes that were in use on the circuit when it failed. Make repairs if necessary, then switch on the appliances or lights one at a time. Check that you are not overloading the circuit – this is the most likely cause of the blown fuse. If the fuse blows again, call an electrician.

Checking a miniature circuit breaker

If the consumer unit is fitted with miniature circuit breakers (MCBs) instead of circuit fuses, it is immediately clear which circuit is affected. The switch will be in the 'off' position or the button will have popped out.

1 Turn off the main switch on the consumer unit.

2 Switch off all appliances or light switches on the affected circuit. If you do not do this, the MCB may trip off again when you reset it.

3 Push the MCB switch to the 'on' position or push in the button. Then turn the main switch back on. Finally check the circuit (see above). If you cannot reset the MCB, call in an electrician to trace the cause of the fault.

Fitting a plug

All electrical appliances sold in the UK must have a factory-fitted plug. However, you may need to fit a replacement plug if the factory-fitted one is damaged. Also, many older appliances in the home still have hand-wired plugs, which may also need replacing over time.

All three-pin plugs are fitted with a cartridge fuse. Most contain a 13amp fuse (colour coded brown) when you buy them, but you should fit a lower-rated fuse if the appliance rating is below 700 watts. Table lamps, for example, usually require a 3amp fuse (colour coded red).

Tools Screwdrivers; sharp knife; wire cutters and strippers; pliers.

Materials Plug; flex; 3amp or 13amp fuse.

1 Unscrew the cover of the new plug and remove it.

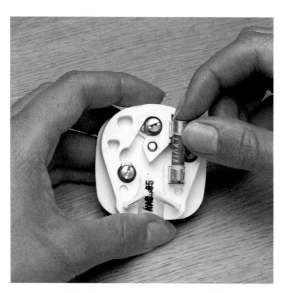

2 Prise out the cartridge fuse if necessary to reveal the terminal. Loosen the screw-down bar that secures the flex if there is one. Plastic jaws grip the flex in some plugs.

3 If you are replacing a hand-wired plug, remove its cover and loosen the terminal screws to release the flex cores from their terminals. Release the flex from the flex grip. Inspect the bare cores. If they appear damaged, cut them off and strip off some core insulation to expose undamaged wires ready for reconnection to the new plug.

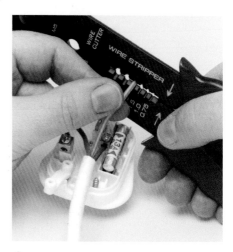

4 If you are replacing a factory-fitted plug, cut through the flex close to the plug body. Strip back the outer sheath and cut the individual cores to the right length to reach their terminals in the new plug. For some plugs all the cores have to be the same length, for others they have to be different lengths. Check that the prepared cores are long enough to reach their terminals with the flex sheath held in the flex grip.

SAFETY STANDARDS

Buy plugs marked 'Made to British Standard BS1363', and fuses made to BS1362. Fit tough rubber plugs to power tools and to garden equipment, to prevent them being damaged if dropped.

If you are discarding a moulded-on plug, cut through the flex close to the plug body. Then deform the pins with hammer blows so the plug, if found, cannot be inserted in a socket outlet and cause the user to receive a shock.

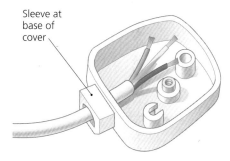

Sleeve at base of cover

Alternatively **Alternatively** With screw-down stud terminals, remove the stud and wind the bare end of the core clockwise round the threaded peg. Screw the stud down to trap the wires in place.

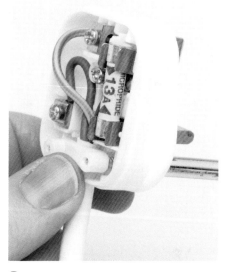

5 Tough rubber plugs designed for use on power tools have a hole in the plug cover through which the flex passes before being connected to the plug terminals.

6 Connect each flex core to its correct terminal. The **BR**own (live) core goes to the **B**ottom **R**ight terminal, the **BL**ue (neutral) core to the **B**ottom **L**eft terminal, and the earth core in three-core flex (green-and-yellow) to the top terminal.

8 Arrange the cores in their channels in the plug body and place the flex sheath in the cord grip. If the plug has nylon jaws, press the flex in between them. If it has a screw-down bar, undo one screw, position the flex in the grip, swing the bar back over it and screw it down securely. Fit the fuse.

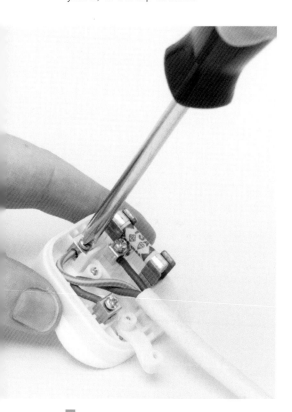

7 With pillar-type terminals, loosen the terminal screw and insert the bare end of the core in the hole. Tighten the screw to trap it in place. Plugs with this type of terminal often have loose pins; remove these from the plug first if it makes connecting the cores easier.

9 Replace the plug cover and make sure that it is firmly screwed together.

Extending a flex

Never join lengths of flex by twisting together the cores and binding the join with insulating tape. It may overheat and start a fire.

If you have to extend a flex, use a one-piece connector to make a permanent joint, or use a two-part connector if you want to be able to separate the joint. This must have three pins for connecting appliances that use three-core flex. Two-pin connectors are used mainly for connecting double-insulated garden power tools (marked with the symbol ▣) to extension leads.

Tools *Screwdrivers; sharp knife; wire cutters and strippers; pliers.*

Materials *Flex connector; length of flex fitted with a plug.*

1 Unscrew the connector cover and remove it. Prepare the ends of both flexes for connection by stripping back the insulating sheath and checking that the cores will be long enough to reach their brass terminals. Strip about 15mm of coloured insulation from each core.

2 Lift out the brass barrel terminals and loosen all the terminal screws.

3 Push the cores into the terminals so that they match – brown to brown in one terminal, green-and-yellow to green-and-yellow in the second, and blue to blue in the third. Tighten all the terminal screws.

4 Loosen one screw and remove the other from each cord grip so you can swing the bar aside.

5 Fit the brass barrel terminals in their slots and position each flex sheath beneath its cord grip.

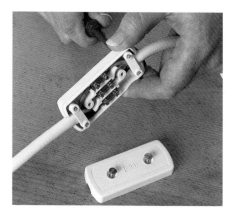

6 Replace the cord grip screws and tighten them to grip the flex sheaths securely. Fit and screw on the cover.

REPLACING A HALOGEN BULB

Gently squeeze together the two ends of the metal circlip just visible around the inner edge of the fitting. Remove the circlip and the bulb will be released from its housing and will dangle out of the hole in the ceiling. Carefully pull the bulb away from the plug at the end of the wire then connect the new bulb. Push the bulb back up into the ceiling recess and replace the circlip to hold it in place.

Replacing a pendant lampholder

Old lampholders crack and perish after a few years and are best replaced. If the flex connections in a pendant lampholder pull away from their terminals and stop the light working, they simply need reconnecting.

If the lampholder is a metal one without an earth terminal, replace it with an earthed one, or with a plastic lampholder if the flex has no earth core. You must use three-core flex with metal lampholders.

Tools *Insulated screwdrivers, one with a small, fine tip; wire cutters and strippers; pliers.*

Materials *New lampholder if replacing.*

1 Turn off the power at the consumer unit or fuse box, remove the lighting circuit fuse or switch off the MCB (page 92). Restore the power to the other circuits and test the light to make sure the power is off.

2 Remove the bulb and unscrew the shade ring that holds the lampshade. With a very old lampholder, you may have to break the ring by crushing it with pliers. Remove the shade and unscrew the top cover.

3 Using an insulated screwdriver, unhook the flex cores from the lugs on the body of the lampholder.

4 With the fine screwdriver, undo the terminal screws enough to draw out the flex cores. Remove the lampholder and cover from the flex.

5 Thread the new cover onto the flex and attach the flex cores tightly to the terminals – it does not matter which each goes to. Hook the flex cores over the support lugs. Screw the lampholder cover on. Refit the shade, shade ring and bulb.

6 Replace the circuit fuse or switch on the MCB and restore the power.

The parts of a lampholder

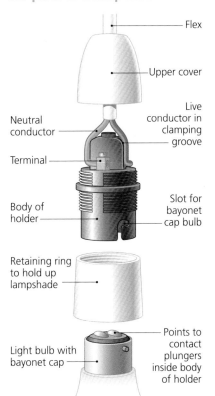

- Flex
- Upper cover
- Neutral conductor
- Live conductor in clamping groove
- Terminal
- Body of holder
- Slot for bayonet cap bulb
- Retaining ring to hold up lampshade
- Light bulb with bayonet cap
- Points to contact plungers inside body of holder

Plumbing and heating

Plumbing emergencies – what to do if:

Water pours from the loft

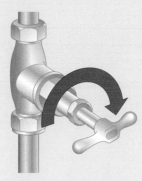

1 Turn the main stoptap off (clockwise). It is usually close to the kitchen sink (if you can't turn it off, see right). Put buckets under the leaks, then turn on all the cold taps in the house and flush all the WCs to drain the cold water storage cistern.

2 Find the cause of the trouble. It may be a burst pipe in the loft or a cistern overflow caused by a blocked overflow pipe.

No water comes from a tap

1 If no water flows from the kitchen sink cold tap, check that the main stoptap is open. If it is, call your water supply company. You will find the number under **'Water'** in the phone book.

2 If no water flows from other taps, check the cold water cistern. It may have emptied because of a jammed ballvalve. If it is empty, move the float arm sharply up and down to free the valve.

Alternatively In frosty weather there may be an ice plug blocking a supply pipe. If the kitchen cold tap is working, check the flow into the cold water cistern by pressing down the ballvalve. If there is no inflow, the rising main is frozen, probably in the loft between the ceiling and cistern inlet.

3 If the cistern is filling, check the bathroom taps. If there is no flow from one tap, its supply pipe from the cistern is frozen.

4 To thaw a pipe, strip off any lagging from the affected part and apply hot water bottles. If a pipe is difficult to get at, blow warm air onto it with a hair dryer.

WARNING Do not use a blowtorch to defrost a frozen pipe. It may cause a fire, or melt the solder in a pipe joint and cause another leak.

Hot water cylinder leaks

1 Turn off the gatevalve (clockwise) on the supply pipe from the cold water cistern to the hot water cylinder. If there is no gatevalve, turn off the main stoptap and turn on all the taps to empty the cistern. (This will not empty the hot water cylinder, but will stop water from flowing into it.)

2 Switch off the boiler and the immersion heater, if fitted.

3 Connect a hose to the cylinder drain valve (near the base of the cylinder where the supply pipe from the cold water cistern enters). Put the other end of the hose into an outside drain.

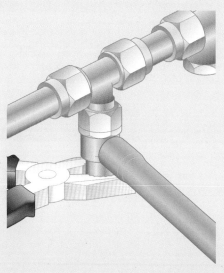

4 Open up the drain valve with pliers (or a special drain valve key).

5 Get the hot water cylinder repaired or replaced by a plumber.

You cannot turn off the water

If you cannot turn off the water at the main stoptap, tie up the float arm in the cold water cistern to stop it filling, turn on all the taps (except the kitchen cold tap) and flush the WCs. Then call an emergency plumber.

There is also an outdoor stoptap – usually under a small metal plate in the pavement or driveway outside (see page 104). If you cannot find or turn off the indoor stoptap, then use this tap. You will need a special stoptap key with a long handle – or if desperate, lie on the ground and put your arm down the hole to reach the tap with a spanner or pliers.

Other plumbing problems

Trade organisations

Association of Plumbing and Heating Contractors
14 Ensign House
Ensign Business Centre
Westwood Way
Coventry
CV4 8JA
Tel: 024 7647 0626
Fax: 024 7647 0942
Email: enquiries@aphc.co.uk
www.aphc.co.uk

Institute of Plumbing and Heating Engineering
64 Station Lane
Hornchurch
Essex
RM12 6NB
Tel: 01708 472791
Fax: 01708 448987
Email: info@iphe.org.uk
www.iphe.org.uk

CORGI (Council for Registered Gas Installers)
1 Elmwood
Chineham Business Park
Crockford Lane
Basingstoke
RG24 8WG
Tel: 0870 401 2200
Fax: 0870 401 2600
Email: enquiries@corgi-group.com
www.corgi-group.com

How water is supplied to the home

Whether for home improvements, or for tackling emergencies, it is important to know what type of water system you have, and where to find all the relevant system controls.

The cold water supply

There are two types of cold water supply in British homes: direct and indirect.

In a direct cold water supply, branch pipes from the rising main lead directly to all the cold taps and WC cisterns in the house. This means that you can drink cold water from any tap. A pipe from the rising main will usually feed a storage cistern in the loft – the reservoir that feeds the hot water cylinder. A direct cold water system is simpler and cheaper to install than an indirect system.

Most British homes have an indirect system. The rising main feeds the cold tap at the kitchen sink (and possibly pipes to a washing machine and an outside tap). This water is clean drinking water. It then continues up to a cold water storage tank in the roof, which supplies all other taps, the WCs and the hot water cylinder.

There are advantages to an indirect system: water from a cold water storage cistern gives even water pressure, which produces quieter plumbing and less wear and tear on washers and valves. Leaks are also less likely, and any leak that does occur will be less damaging than one from a pipe under mains pressure.

Also, water from a cistern is warmer than mains water, so less hot water is needed for washing and bathing. It also reduces condensation on WC cisterns. And if the house supply is temporarily cut off – for work on the mains, for example – there is a supply of stored water available for use.

Rising main The service pipe enters the house, usually close to the kitchen sink (but sometimes under the stairs or in a garage), and from there is known as the rising main. A stoptap for cutting off the house water supply should be fitted where the pipe enters the house. The rising main is usually a 15mm diameter pipe, but in areas where mains pressure is low, 22mm pipe is used.

Water meter If the property has a water meter, it will be installed outside the property boundary, between the mains and the outdoor stoptap.

To cold water cistern (or direct draw-off points)

Rising main with indoor stoptap

Guard pipe

Water mains

Communication pipe

Outdoor stoptap

Service pipe

Water mains The water supply to most British homes is provided by the local water supply company, through iron or heavy plastic water mains.

Communication pipe From the mains, takes the water to the water company's stoptap – a control valve about 1m below the ground at or near the boundary of each property.

Outdoor stoptap The stoptap, which is turned with a long key, is at the bottom of an earthenware guard pipe under a small metal cover, set into the surface of the garden or the public footpath outside. In older properties, this may be the only place where the water can be turned off.

Service pipe From the water company's stoptap, a service pipe carries water into the house. The pipe should meander slightly in the trench to allow for ground movement, which would otherwise pull on the fittings at each end. To avoid frost damage, it should be at least 750mm and not more than 1.35m below ground.

Where the waste water goes

If you live in a house built before the mid-1960s, you probably have a two pipe drainage system; newer houses have one drain pipe – a single stack system.

Whatever the drainage system, every bath, basin or sink in the house is fitted with a trap – a bend in the outlet pipe below the plughole. This holds sufficient water to stop gases from the drains entering the house and causing an unpleasant smell. The trap has some means of access for clearing blockages. All WC pans have built-in traps.

Below ground, the household waste pipes or drains are channelled through an inspection chamber near the house to form the main drain, which runs into the water company's sewer.

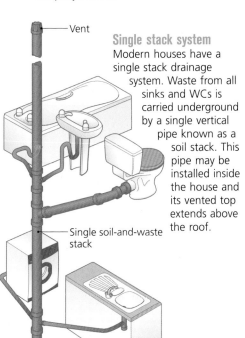

— Vent

Single stack system

Modern houses have a single stack drainage system. Waste from all sinks and WCs is carried underground by a single vertical pipe known as a soil stack. This pipe may be installed inside the house and its vented top extends above the roof.

— Single soil-and-waste stack

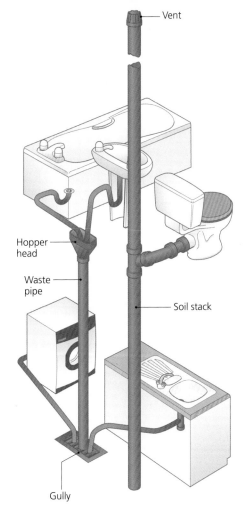

— Vent

Hopper head —

Waste pipe —

— Soil stack

Gully

Two pipe system

Most houses built before the mid-1960s have what is known as a two pipe drainage system for waste water disposal.

A vertical soil stack fixed to an outside wall carries waste from upstairs WCs to an underground drain. The open top of the soil stack – the vent – extends above the eaves and allows the escape of sewer gases. It is protected from birds with a metal or wire mesh guard. Ground floor WCs have an outlet direct into the underground drain.

A second outside pipe – the waste pipe – takes used water from upstairs baths, basins and showers via an open hopper head to empty into a ground-level gully. Water from the kitchen sink also runs into a gully.

Cutting off the water supply

In many homes, only the kitchen tap is fed from the rising main; others are fed from the cold water cistern. It depends whether the plumbing system is direct or indirect (page 104).

Taps fed from the cistern

1 To isolate a hot or cold tap supplied from the cistern, turn off the gatevalve on the supply pipe from the cistern. If a service valve (see right) is fitted in the pipe to the tap, turn it off with a screwdriver.

2 Keep turning the tap until the water stops flowing.

Alternatively If there is no gatevalve or service valve on the pipe, you will have to drain the cistern.

Draining the cistern

1 Tie the ballvalve arm to a piece of wood laid across the cistern (in the same way as over a WC cistern, page 118). This stops the flow from the mains.

2 Turn on the bathroom cold taps until the water stops flowing, then turn on the hot taps – very little water will flow from them. (You need not turn off the boiler, as the hot water cylinder will not be drained.)

Taps fed from the rising main

Turn off the main indoor stoptap, then turn on the mains-fed tap until the water stops.

Draining the rising main

You, or a plumber, may want to drain the rising main to take a branch pipe from it or to repair the main stoptap. If there is a drain valve above the stoptap, fit a short piece of hose to its outlet and open it with a drain valve key or pliers. Catch the water, usually only a litre or two, in a bucket.

Service valve Small isolating valves can be found in pipework leading to taps, ballvalves or appliances. They are closed and opened **by a half turn only** with a screwdriver, allowing you to stop the water flow for repairs. A similar valve with a small lever handle and a threaded outlet is used to control the flow to the flexible supply hoses of a washing machine or dishwasher.

HELPFUL TIP

A stoptap that has been open for a long time may be jammed. To guard against this, close and open the stoptap fully twice a year. After opening it, give the handle a quarter turn towards closure. This prevents jamming without affecting water flow. If a stoptap is difficult to turn, apply a few drops of penetrating oil round the spindle base or give it a squirt with WD40 and leave for ten minutes before turning the handle again. Repeat as necessary.

Turning off the outdoor stoptap

You may need to turn off the outdoor stoptap (see page 104) if the indoor one is broken, jammed or has a leak from the spindle. Stoptap keys can be bought from plumbers' merchants, but **first check** the type needed – the tap may have a crutch handle or a square spindle.

Repairing a burst pipe

Metal pipes are more likely to suffer frost damage than plastic pipes. Copper and stainless steel pipes are less vulnerable than softer lead pipes.

As an ice plug forms, it expands and may split the pipe or force open a joint. When the ice melts, the pipe or fitting leaks. A split copper or plastic pipe can be temporarily repaired with a proprietary burst-pipe repair clamp (right). In an emergency, a pipe not under mains pressure can be patched with a length of garden hose.

Call a plumber to make a permanent repair as soon as possible.

For lead piping, use a tape-repair kit for a strong repair that will allow you to restore the water supply until a plumber can make a permanent repair – or better still, completely replace the old lead pipe.

Patching a split branch pipe

1 Cut a piece of garden hose that is long enough to cover the pipe for at least 50mm beyond the area of damage in each direction. Split the hose along its length.

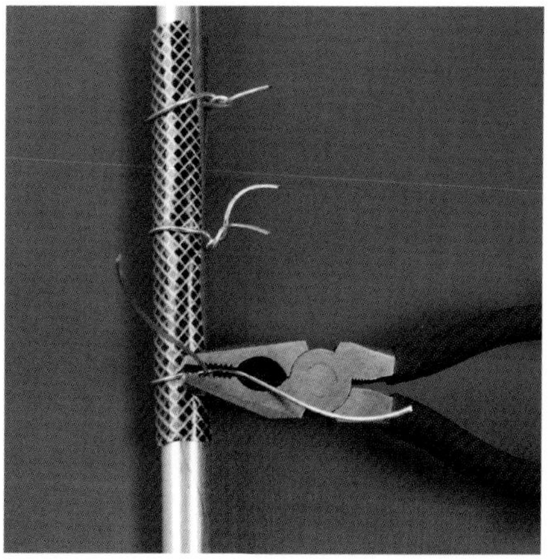

2 Wrap the hose round the pipe to cover the damage and secure it with three loops of strong wire. Twist the loops closed tightly with pliers.

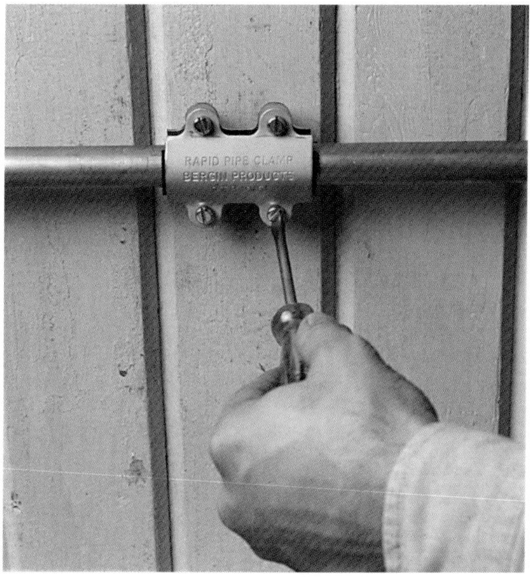

Alternatively Fit an emergency pipe repair clamp (sold in plumbers' merchants and some hardware stores) and tighten the screws fully with a screwdriver.

How taps work

All taps work in much the same way – a rotating handle opens and closes a valve inside the body of the tap. Traditional taps, such as the rising spindle, use a system of nuts and screws to open the valve, but modern taps use rotating discs instead.

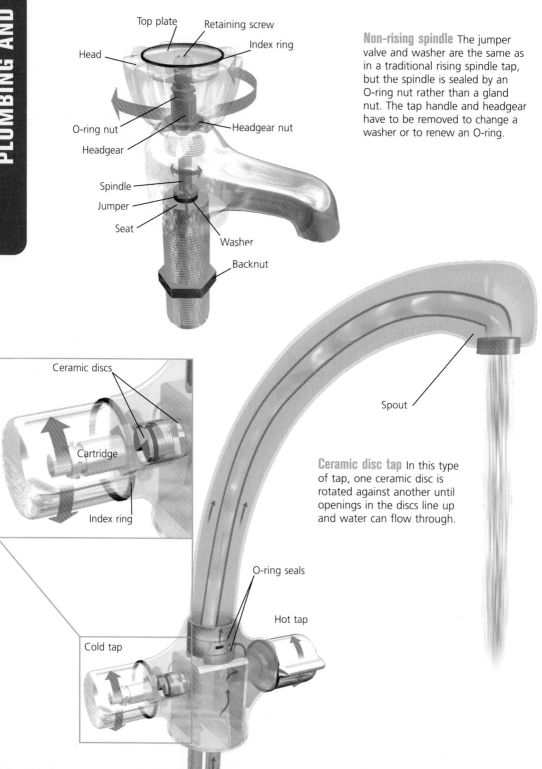

Top plate
Retaining screw
Head
Index ring
O-ring nut
Headgear nut
Headgear
Spindle
Jumper
Seat
Washer
Backnut

Ceramic discs
Cartridge
Index ring
O-ring seals
Cold tap
Hot tap
Spout

Non-rising spindle The jumper valve and washer are the same as in a traditional rising spindle tap, but the spindle is sealed by an O-ring nut rather than a gland nut. The tap handle and headgear have to be removed to change a washer or to renew an O-ring.

Ceramic disc tap In this type of tap, one ceramic disc is rotated against another until openings in the discs line up and water can flow through.

Mixer taps The only difference between a mixer tap and a non-rising spindle tap (left) is that the hot and cold water share the same outlet. In a kitchen mixer the spout has two separate water channels for hot and cold water just like the ceramic disc tap (below left). The two jets of water mix only as they leave the outlet because it is against water regulations to mix cold water from the mains (as it is on all kitchen taps) with hot water from a water cylinder. This is because the pressure on the mains supply can vary and under certain conditions could draw back non-drinking water from the cylinder into the mains supply.

Mixer units for use on baths and basins can mix water supplies within the tap body as long as the cold water is coming from a water tank, not directly from the rising main supply.

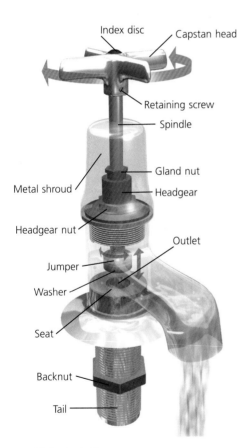

Index disc

Capstan head

Retaining screw

Spindle

Gland nut

Metal shroud

Headgear

Headgear nut

Outlet

Jumper

Washer

Seat

Backnut

Tail

Rising spindle The jumper valve is in the shape of a rod and plate, and the washer is attached to the base of the plate. When changing a washer, the handle is lifted off with the headgear. When adjusting the gland nut, the handle has to be removed so that the bell-shaped cover can be pulled off out of the way.

Repairing a dripping tap

A dripping tap usually means that the tap washer needs renewing, but can also be caused by a damaged valve seating. If the drip is from a mixer spout, renew both tap washers.

Tools *Adjustable spanner; cloth for padding jaws of spanner; old screwdriver (for prising). Possibly also one small spanner (normally 8mm); screwdrivers.*

Materials *Replacement washer or a washer-and-jumper valve unit; alternatively, a washer-and-seating set; petroleum jelly. Possibly also penetrating oil or WD40.*

Removing the headgear

1 Cut off the water supply (page 106). Make sure the tap is turned fully on, and put the plug into the plughole to stop any small parts falling down the waste pipe.

2 Unscrew or lever off the cover of a non-rising spindle tap to expose the retaining screw. Remove the screw and put it in a safe place. Remove the head.

Alternatively With a rising spindle tap, prise off the index disc and remove the retaining screw to release the capstan from the spindle. Use a spanner (or wrench) wrapped in cloth to unscrew the metal shroud and lift it away from the headgear nut.

TAPS

3 Undo the headgear nut with a spanner. Be sure to hold the tap body firmly to prevent the tap from turning and fracturing the pipework attached to it. Do not force the nut, if it is stiff.

4 If the nut is difficult to turn, apply penetrating oil or WD40 round the joint, wait about ten minutes to give it time to soak in, then try again. You may have to make several applications.

Fitting the washer

1 Prise off the washer with a screwdriver. If there is a small nut holding it in place, unscrew it with a spanner (normally 8mm). If it is difficult to undo, put penetrating oil round it and try again when it has soaked in. Then prise off the washer.

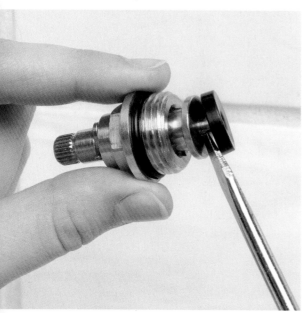

Alternatively If the nut is impossible to remove, you can replace both the jumper valve and washer in one unit.

2 After fitting a new washer or washer and jumper, grease the threads on the base of the tap with petroleum jelly before reassembling.

Repairing the valve seating

Washer-and-jumper valve unit
Plastic seating
Valve seat

When renewing a washer, inspect the valve seat inside the tap body. If it is scaled or scored by grit, the seal between washer and seat will not be effective even with a new washer.

The simplest repair is with a washer-and-seating set. This has a plastic seat to fit into the valve seat, and a washer-and-jumper valve unit to fit into the headgear.

When the tap is turned off, the plastic seating is forced firmly into place. It may take a few days for the new seating to give a completely watertight fit.

Cleaning or replacing ceramic discs

Positioned in the body of the ceramic disc tap (page 108) is a cartridge containing a pair of ceramic discs, each with two holes in it.

One disc is fixed in position; the other rotates when the handle is turned. As the movable disc rotates, the holes in it line up with the holes in the fixed one and water flows through them. When the tap is turned off the movable disc rotates so that the holes no longer align.

Dealing with a dripping tap

If a scratched ceramic disc is causing the leak, the entire cartridge must be replaced: left-handed for a hot tap or right-handed for a cold tap. Remove the old cartridge and take it with you when buying a replacement to make sure it is the correct size and 'hand'. Ceramic taps can also drip at the base of the cartridge if the seal has perished. Replace it if necessary.

Checking discs in a ceramic disc mixer tap

1 Turn off the water supply. Pull off the tap handles (it may be necessary to unscrew a small retaining screw on each) and use a spanner to unscrew the headgear section.

2 Carefully remove the ceramic cartridges, keeping hot and cold separate. Check both cartridges for dirt and wear and tear.

3 If the cartridges are worn, replace with identical parts for the tap unit. Make sure the hot and cold cartridges are fitted into the correct taps.

4 If the cartridges are dirty, clean them with a damp cloth. Replace the rubber seal, if it is worn. Replace the cartridge in the tap unit, fitting the hot and cold cartridges into the appropriate taps.

Curing a leak from a spindle or spout

Leakage from the body of the tap – from round the spindle, the base of a swivel spout, or the diverter knob on a shower mixer tap – may indicate a faulty gland or O-ring seal.

This sort of leak is most likely to occur on a kitchen cold tap with a bell-shaped cover and visible spindle.

On a modern tap, especially one with a shrouded head, there is an O-ring seal instead of a gland, and it rarely needs replacing. However, an O-ring seal may occasionally become worn.

Tools *Adjustable spanner, screwdrivers; old screwdriver for prising; two small wooden blocks about 10mm deep (such as spring clothes pegs).*

Materials *Packing material – PTFE tape. Possibly also silicone grease; O-rings (and possibly washers) of the correct size – take the old ones with you when buying, or give the make of tap.*

Adjusting the gland

There is no need to cut off the water supply to the tap.

1 With the tap turned off, undo the small screw that secures the capstan handle and put it in a safe place (it is very easily lost), then remove the handle. If there is no screw, the handle should pull off.

2 Remove the bell-shaped cover to reveal the gland nut – the highest nut on the spindle. Tighten the nut about half a turn with a spanner.

3 Turn the tap on by temporarily slipping the handle back on, then check whether there is still a leak from the spindle. If there is not, turn the gland nut another quarter turn and reassemble the tap. Do not overtighten the gland nut, or the tap will be hard to turn off.

4 If there is still a leak, give another half turn and check again. If the gland continues leaking after you have adjusted it as far as possible, you will need to repack the gland.

Replacing the packing

1 With the tap turned off and the handle and cover removed, use a spanner to remove the gland nut and lift it out.

2 Pick out the old packing with a small screwdriver. Replace it with PTFE tape pulled into a thin string. Pack it in with a screwdriver, then replace the gland nut and reassemble the tap.

Renewing the O-ring on a shrouded-head tap

1 Cut off the water supply to the tap (page 106) and remove the tap handle and headgear in the same way as for renewing a washer (page 109).

2 Hold the headgear between your fingers and turn the spindle clockwise to unscrew and remove the washer unit.

3 Prise out the O-ring at the top of the washer unit with a screwdriver or penknife. Smear the new O-ring with silicone grease, fit it in position, and reassemble the tap.

RELEASING THE SPINDLE

A non-rising spindle tap may have a circlip keeping the spindle in place. After removing the headgear, lever out the circlip so that you can reach the worn O-rings.

Renewing O-rings on a kitchen mixer tap

1 With both taps turned off, remove any retaining screw found behind the spout. If there is no screw, turn the spout to line up with the tap body and pull upwards sharply.

2 Note the position of the O-rings (probably two) and remove them.

3 Coat new O-rings of the correct size with silicone grease and fit them in position. Smear the inside of the spout end with petroleum jelly and refit it.

Dealing with a blocked sink

Grease may have built up in the trap and waste pipe, trapping food particles and other debris, or an object may be obstructing the waste pipe.

Tools Possibly a length of wire; sink-waste plunger; sink auger or a length of expanding curtain wire; bucket.

Materials Caustic soda or proprietary chemical or enzyme cleaner; petroleum jelly.

Sink slow to empty

If a sink is slow to empty, smear petroleum jelly on the rim of the plug hole to protect it, and then apply proprietary chemical or enzyme cleaner according to the manufacturer's instructions.

Sink completely blocked

1 If the water will not run away at all, place the sink plunger cup squarely over the plug hole.

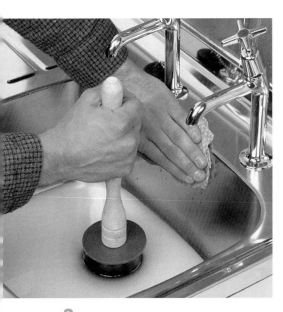

2 Stuff a damp cloth firmly into the overflow opening and hold it there. This stops air escaping through the hole and dissipating the force you build up by plunging. Pump the plunger sharply up and down. If the blockage does not clear, repeat the operation.

3 If plunging fails, replace the sink plug. Put a bucket under the sink and disconnect the trap. Wash it out thoroughly if it is blocked with debris.

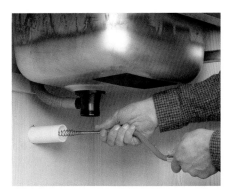

4 If the obstruction is not in the trap, try using a plumber's snake. It is a spiral device that can be hired or bought. Disconnect the blocked pipe from its trap and feed the wire into it. Then turn the handle to rotate the spiral. This drives its cutting head into the blockage and breaks it up.

Alternatively If you have a vacuum cleaner that is designed to cope with liquids, you can use it to try to dislodge a blockage in a sink trap. Press a cloth over the overflow in the sink. Then place the suction tube of the vacuum over the plughole and switch on. This will probably loosen the blockage sufficiently to allow it to be carried away by the water flow through the trap.

Alternatively If you have poured fat into the sink and it has hardened, try warming the pipe with a hair dryer, to melt the grease. Flush plenty of hot water after it.

Other pipe blockages

Washing machines and dishwashers are often plumbed in to feed the under-sink waste trap. Alternatively, they may join the main waste pipe at a T-junction away from the sink. If all your appliances feed into the one trap, you may need to disconnect all the pipes in turn and then clean each one.

Toilets

The basic design of the one-piece toilet has changed little in more than 100 years. Clean water is stored in a cistern above the bowl until the flush is operated. The water is channelled around the rim, rinsing waste matter out of the bowl and via the trap into the drainage system.

The most common problems with WCs are that the WC will not flush, that water runs continuously into the pan or that water runs continuously into the cistern and out through the overflow pipe. Most of these problems are easily fixed.

WC will not flush Check that the flushing lever is still attached to the internal workings of the cistern. Reattach the link (see page 118) or improvise a replacement from a length of thick wire. If the link is still in place, the flap valve may need replacing – this is often the cause if you need to operate the lever several times before the WC will flush.

Continuous flushing When water keeps running into the pan, the siphon may have split or the sealing washer at the base of the siphon

may have perished. Both can be replaced. Alternatively, the cistern may be filling too fast, so that the siphoning action of the flush mechanism cannot be interrupted. A restrictor can be fitted in the float valve to reduce the water flow.

Overflowing cistern Continuous filling may be caused by a faulty float valve or a badly adjusted float arm. Try adjusting the float arm by bending the wire slightly.

Water rising up bowl when flushed If the water does not drain away freely from the bowl it is a sign that the outlet pipe is blocked. Free the blockage with a plunger or auger (see page 116)

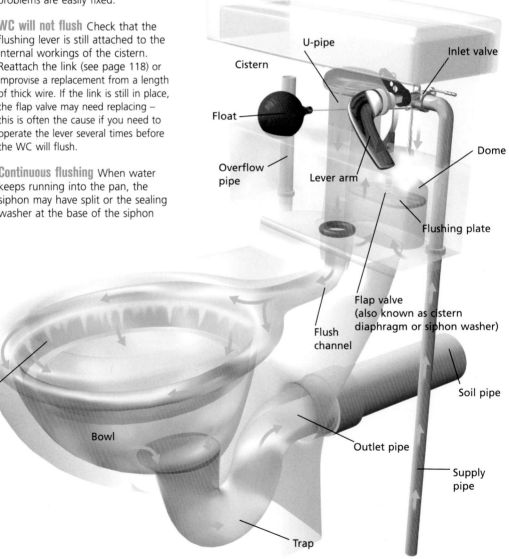

U-pipe

Inlet valve

Cistern

Float

Dome

Overflow pipe

Lever arm

Flushing plate

Flap valve
(also known as cistern
diaphragm or siphon washer)

Flush
channel

Flushing rim

Soil pipe

Bowl

Outlet pipe

Supply pipe

Trap

A push-button or 'European' cistern

Many modern slimline WC cisterns are too small to accommodate a traditional ball float-operated inlet valve and siphon flush mechanism, operated by a lever and float arm (see opposite).

Instead, the inlet valve is either a Torbeck valve – a modified diaphragm type with a very short float arm and miniature float (below) – or an ingenious vertical valve with a float cup that fits round the central column of the valve body. Both are very quiet in operation, although the float-cup valve can be slow to refill the cistern if it is supplied with water from a storage tank, rather than being plumbed in directly to the mains.

In these slimline mechanisms, the traditional siphon flushing method is replaced by a plastic valve-operated flush mechanism that is activated by a top-mounted push button in the cistern lid. The mechanism also incorporates an integral overflow, and if the inlet valve fails for any reason, the water flows over the centre of the flush unit into the toilet bowl. This will be noticed as constantly running water in the toilet bowl and should be repaired as soon as possible.

The push button is in two parts (see box, right) and is linked to a plunger to operate the flush, rather than the conventional wire link and float arm of a traditional flushing mechanism.

CHOOSE A DOUBLE FLUSH SYSTEM TO SAVE WATER

Many modern WCs have a dual-flush cistern, allowing you to choose either a water-conserving short flush or a full flush. Conventional siphon-flush cisterns (far left) have a hole in the side of the dome; if the flush lever is released immediately, the hole lets in air after 4 litres of water have been siphoned. If the control is held down, it temporarily plugs the hole, allowing a double flush.

Push-button WCs may have a button in two parts (above). Depress one part for a low-volume flush and the other (or both, on some models) for a full-volume flush

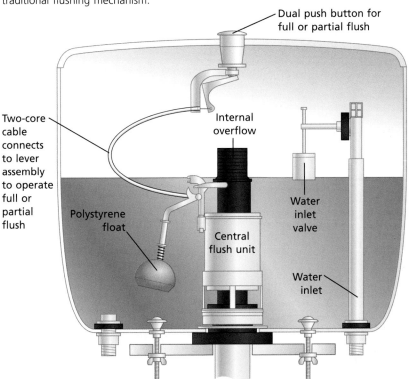

Dual push button for full or partial flush

Two-core cable connects to lever assembly to operate full or partial flush

Polystyrene float

Internal overflow

Water inlet valve

Central flush unit

Water inlet

PLUMBING AND HEATING

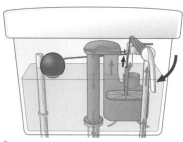

1 An inverted U-pipe is linked to the flush pipe into the pan, and at the other end opens out into a dome (siphon). When the flush is operated, a lift rod raises a plate in the dome and throws water over the U-bend.

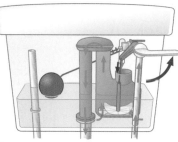

2 Openings in the plate are covered by a plastic flap valve held flat by the weight of the water. As water falls down the flush pipe, it creates a partial vacuum, sucking water through the plate and raising the flap valve.

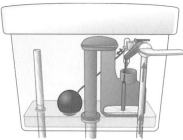

3 The base of the dome is just above the cistern bottom. When the water level falls below the dome base, air breaks the siphonic action and stops the flush. As the cistern refills, the float lifts the inlet valve arm. When the arm reaches the top of its travel, the inlet valve closes off the water entering through the supply pipe. Some cisterns use a quieter Torbeck valve, which has a small cylinder in place of the ball float.

Clearing a blocked toilet

Blockages are a common problem. You can often clear a blockage by pouring several buckets of warm water into the pan, from a height if possible. Alternatively you may need to use a plunger or an auger to dislodge it.

When a toilet is flushed, the two streams of water, one from each side of the rim, should flow equally to meet at the front. The water should leave the pan smoothly, not eddying like a whirlpool. If the cistern is working properly but the bowl fails to clear, something is obstructing either the flush inlet or the pan outlet. If the flush water rises almost to the pan rim, then ebbs away very slowly, there is probably a blockage in the pan outlet (or possibly in the soil stack or drain into which it discharges, see page 119).

Tools *WC plunger. Possibly also flexible drain auger; bucket; mirror; a pair of rubber gloves.*

1 To clear the pan, take the plunger and push it sharply onto the bottom of the pan to cover the outlet. Then pump the handle up and down two or three times. If you don't have a plunger, try using a mop.

2 If this does not clear the pan, use a flexible drain auger to probe the outlet and trap. As you insert the auger, turn it slowly. If you meet hard resistance, turn the auger back and forth to move it past the trap. When you meet soft resistance, push and pull gently to dislodge the blockage. Flush the bowl with a bucket of water.

3 If the blockage persists, you will need to contact a drain-rodding company to get the underground drain checked and cleared.

4 Flush the cistern to check that water is entering the pan properly, with streams from each side of the rim flowing equally to meet at the front.

5 If the flow into the pan is poor or uneven, use a mirror to examine the flushing rim. Use your fingers to dislodge flakes of limescale or debris from the cistern that may be obstructing the flush water.

Replacing a seat

Seats get broken over time, or the brackets may crack – or you may just want to replace an old seat with a new one to brighten up the bathroom. Whatever the reason, replacing a seat is a straightforward job.

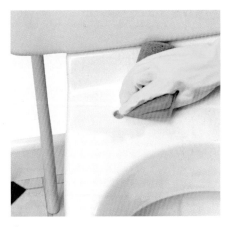

1 Undo the plastic wing-nuts under the rear of the toilet bowl and remove the old seat. Clean around the bolt holes and place the new seat in position.

2 Fit the supplied washers both above and below the bowl, two on each bolt. Finger-tighten the wing-nuts, check the seat is centred and tighten the nuts fully.

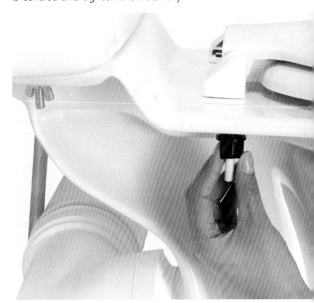

Replacing a broken link to the ball valve

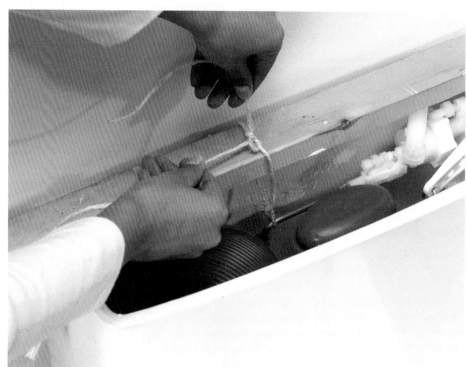

1 Turn off the water supply to the toilet and flush it by pulling up on the rod protruding from the dome of the siphon. If you cannot turn the water off, place a wooden batten across the cistern and tie the ball valve arm up.

2 Remove the broken sections of link from the ends of the rods and discard them. Then fit the new link between the siphon rod and the nylon connector bar.

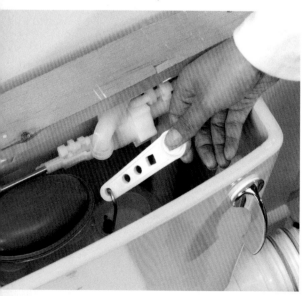

3 Push the other end of the bar onto the lever arm rod. Make sure the lever arm is in the correct 'rest' position, and tighten the retaining screw. Then untie the float from the wooden batten (or turn the water supply back on) and let the cistern refill.

Reconnect the link

If you cannot flush the toilet because the handle is hanging limply, check the connection inside the cistern between the flush lever arm and the siphon lift rod. This S-shaped or C-shaped wire link may have become unhooked. Simply reconnect it to restore the flush action. To do this you may have to slip a finger beneath the siphon unit and push the plate inside up so that the top of the lift rod is exposed.

HELPFUL TIP

Removing limescale from bowl Hold a small mirror under the rim of the bowl to check for limescale deposits. Clean with toilet descaler and brush. Remove an unsightly build-up of limescale from toilet pans using a paste made from citric acid powder and water. Lower the level in the trap by using a mop or brush to push some water round the bend, then leave it blocking the pan. Brush the paste onto the ring of limescale and leave it overnight. Repeat as necessary. The paste also works well on scale beneath the rim of the pan.

Clearing blocked drains

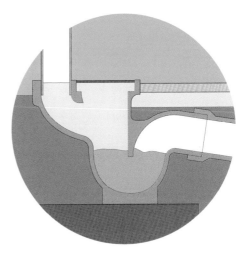

Clearing debris from a gully
Water spilling out of a garden gully (above) suggests a blocked trap below ground level. Remove the gully grating and scoop out the debris by hand, wearing heavy-duty PVC gloves. Then flush the gully through with water to clear any remaining debris and discourage another blockage from forming.

Removing a drain cover
Often the hardest part of unblocking a drain is getting the metal cover off the inspection chamber (manhole). Lever the edge up with a spade or bolster chisel. If it won't budge, tap around the edges with a hammer to break the rust seal. If the grab bars are intact, tie a loop of rope through each one. Pass a length of wood through the loops and lever off the cover.

Clearing a blocked drain
You will need a set of drain rods to clear a blockage in your drainage pipes. Screw two or three rods together and fit the rubber plunger disc to one end. Feed rods into the drain, adding rods until you can reach and dislodge the blockage. Be sure to rotate the rods clockwise or they will unscrew and be lost in the drain. If the plunger does not work, pull out the rods and fit a corkscrew head to pull the obstruction out.

Testing drains
If the drains are not blocked but there is a persistently foul smell, contact the environmental health department at your local authority office for advice.

TOILETS AND DRAINS

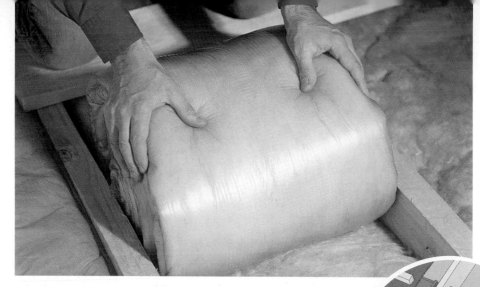

How to keep the heat in

If you don't insulate your loft and your heating pipes, you will waste money by losing heat. This is a simple DIY task that can save you pounds.

Check the insulation already in your loft and add another layer of insulation blanket if what you have is less than 100mm thick. The current Building Regulations require a minimum of 200mm of loft insulation in new houses, so adding an extra layer will bring your property up to present-day standards.

Where plumbing pipes run across the loft floor, double up their protection against frost by insulating them in the usual way (see opposite) and then placing the loft insulation over them. Always keep electricity cables above the insulation wherever possible, so they can't overheat.

Remember the hatch
Tape a piece of insulation blanket to the upper side of the loft hatch and fit self-adhesive foam draughtproofing around the edges of the opening, to prevent heat from the room below escaping into the roof.

PROTECT YOUR HANDS
Because glass fibre can irritate the skin, buy insulation blanket that's wrapped in a thin layer of plastic to make it more pleasant to handle.

Allow breathing space
Keep loft insulation blanket away from the eaves by fitting proprietary plastic ventilator trays between the joists. If the eaves ventilation is blocked, moist air rising from the house will condense within the cold loft space and settle as moisture on the roof timbers. This condensation can cause the wood to rot, and may also saturate the insulation and spoil the plaster and finish on the ceilings of upstairs rooms.

Fast and loose
If the space between your joists varies, as it may in older homes, or if your loft is an awkward shape, insulation blanket may not fit neatly, so lay loose-fill material instead. You can use vermiculite granules (below) or loose mineral wool, both of which can be pushed into hard-to-reach parts of the roof space with a broom. Plastic ventilator trays will stop the granules being lost down a cavity wall if it is open at the top.

Stop draughts blowing granules into heaps by laying them level with the tops of the joists; you can then cover them with

sheets of building paper, stapled over the joists. Don't use polythene; it will trap water vapour and cause condensation.

Keep the tank warm

Don't insulate the loft floor under the cold-water storage tank; a little warm air from the room below should be allowed to rise around the base of the tank, helping to prevent it from freezing in very cold weather. Instead, make as tight a seal as possible between the loft floor insulation and the insulation around the tank itself, so that heat is trapped below the tank rather than being lost into the roof space.

Warming the loft

Insulate the underside of the roof slope if you want a warm loft to use as a playroom, for example. You need to maintain a ventilation gap immediately below the roof covering to prevent any risk of condensation, so use insulation 50mm thick and don't push it against the underside of the slates or tiles. Slabs of mineral wool are stiff enough to wedge between the rafters and stay in place without support, but strips of 50mm-thick insulation blanket will need to be held up by string wound between nails driven into the rafter sides. **Line the roof slope** with hardboard or plasterboard if you want to conceal the insulation and achieve a neater look.

Keeping the pipes warm

Hot and cold water pipes that are exposed to the cold in a loft should be lagged to prevent winter freeze-ups.

Examine the pipes in your loft or any that run along outside walls in unheated rooms. Replace old insulation on these vulnerable pipes with new split-sleeve foam insulation. Following a spate of harsh winters, the manufacturers have increased its wall thickness so it can cope with lower temperatures for longer.

Cut insulation for a neat fit

Make 45° cuts in the new insulation with scissors or a sharp bread knife so that you can form neat joins at elbows and tees (below). Use PVC insulating tape to keep the joints tightly closed and avoid a freeze-up.

Shape a length of insulation to encase a pipe with a gentler bend, such as a vent pipe, by making a series of wedge-shaped nicks in it. The insulation will then fit snugly round the curve. Tape the joints to keep them closed.

Alternatives for awkward places

Where you can't easily fit split-sleeve foam insulation, such as around a gatevalve, wrap the pipe and fitting in hessian-based hair felt – available in rolls from plumbers' merchants. Overlap each turn by 50 per cent so the insulation is doubled in thickness, but don't pull it too tightly or you will squeeze all the air out and reduce its insulating value. Use wire or string to secure the cut ends.

Alternatively, buy self-adhesive foam wrap which comes on a roll, usually 5m or 10m long. Peel off the backing paper and wind the material round the pipes. Overlap the tape as you wind, especially at bends.

Polyurethane foam filler, which comes in aerosol form, is ideal for insulating pipes in inaccessible places such as where they pass through walls. Squirt the foam into the gap, leave it to expand and set hard, then trim off any excess with a sharp knife.

Looking after radiators

If radiators are hot at the bottom and cold at the top, they need bleeding. Keep an eye on the inlet valves, too. A slow leak is easily fixed, but can damage nearby flooring if left to drip.

Bleeding a radiator

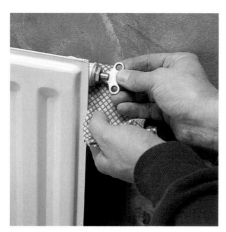

Use a radiator drain key – obtainable from any hardware store – to release air from the system.

Or a flat tip screwdriver On some radiators, a flat tip screwdriver may be required instead of a key. In either case, turn anticlockwise – **no more than a quarter turn** – and hold a cloth directly under the valve to catch any dirty water. Air should vent from the valve, making a hissing noise. When water starts to come out, close the valve and wipe the area dry.

Combined bleed screw

You can buy a small gadget for bleeding radiators which has an integral container for catching any drips.

No need to dismantle the leaking joint

Leaks can occur between the valve tail (the short pipe to which the valve is connected) and the threaded inlet to the radiator itself. This can often be cured with a smear of silicone leak sealant. Run the radiator hot to dry out the leak, then apply the sealant. The leaking water will start it setting immediately, but you should leave the heat on for at least 2 hours to get a total seal.

Repack the gland
Radiator valves, especially cheaper ones, often weep round the spindles. Before replacing the valve, it is worth trying to repack the gland to cure the problem. Turn the valve off, remove the plastic handle and undo the small gland nut at the base of the spindle. Wrap some PTFE tape around the spindle and then push it down into the gap between spindle and valve with a small screwdriver. Add a little silicone grease round the spindle, then replace the nut and handle.

Useful contacts

Electricity

Electrical Contractors Association
ESCA House, 34 Palace Court
London W2 4HY
Tel: 020 7313 4800
Fax: 020 7221 7344
Email:
electricalcontractors@eca.co.uk
www.eca.co.uk

National Inspection Council for Electrical Installation Inspecting (NICEIC)
Warwick House
Houghton Hall Park
Houghton Regis
Dunstable
Bedfordshire LU5 5ZX
Consumer helpline: 0870 013 0382
Tel: 01582 531000
Fax: 01582 531010
Email: enquiries@niceic.com
www.niceic.org.uk

Gas, Plumbing and Heating

CORGI (Council for Registered Gas Installers)
1 Elmwood
Chineham Park
Crockford Lane
Basingstoke RG24 8WG
Tel: 0870 401 2200
Fax: 0870 401 2600
Email: enquiries@corgi-group.com
www.corgi-group.com

Association of Plumbing and Heating Contractors
14 Ensign House
Ensign Business Centre
Westwood Way
Coventry CV4 8JA
Tel: 024 7647 0626
Fax: 024 7647 0942
Email: enquiries@aphc.co.uk
www.aphc.co.uk

Institute of Plumbing and Heating Engineering
64 Station Lane
Hornchurch
Essex
RM12 6NB
Tel: 01708 472791
Fax: 01708 448987
Email: info@iphe.org.uk
www.iphe.org.uk

Security

British Security Industry Association
Security House
Barbourne Road
Worcester WR1 1RS
Tel: 01905 21464
Fax: 01905 613625
Email: info@bsia.co.uk
www.bsia.co.uk

Master Locksmith's Association
5D Great Central Way
Woodford Halse
Daventry NN11 3PZ
Tel: 0800 783 1498
Fax: 01327 262539
Email:
enquiries@locksmiths.co.uk
www.locksmiths.co.uk

Decorating

Painting and Decorating Association
32 Coton Road
Nuneaton
Warwickshire CV11 5TW
Tel: 024 7635 3776
Fax: 024 7635 4513
Email: info@paintingdecorating association.co.uk
www.paintingdecorating association.co.uk

Damp, rot and infestation

British Wood Preserving and Damp-proofing Association
1 Gleneagles House
Vernongate
South Street
Derby DE1 1UP
Tel: 01332 225100
Fax: 01332 225101
Email: info@bwpda.co.uk
www.bwpda.co.uk

British Pest Control Association
1 Gleneagles House
Vernongate
South Street
Derby DE1 1UP
Tel: 0870 609 2687
Fax: 01332 295904
Email: enquiry@bpca.org.uk
www.bpca.org.uk

Advice on the internet

There are many sites offering DIY and appliance repair advice on the internet. Many are linked to specific products or outlets and many are American sites, giving advice (particularly on plumbing and electrics) that does not conform to British safety standards. For impartial, UK-based advice, these are some of the best.

www.bbc.co.uk/homes/diy
Very informative, with advice on most DIY jobs.

www.diydoctor.org.uk/home.htm
Tips and tricks of the trade, information on products and details of local tradespeople and specialists.

www.diyfixit.co.uk
Information on general building, plumbing, electrics and more.

www.easy-diy.co.uk
A comprehensive site that offers advice on products and services.

www.finddiy.co.uk
An excellent starting point, with lots of links to other sites, plus information on tools, equipment and tradespeople.

www.homepro.com
Unusual style ideas as well as down-to-earth DIY, legal and financial advice and a guide to using contractors.

All about your home

Use this page to note down when boilers and other appliances need their annual service and to keep the names and contact details of tradespeople you have used and would use again.

Annual services due dates

Boiler:

Gas fire:

Chimney sweeping:

Recommended contractors

Decorator

Plumber

Electrician

CORGI-registered gas and boiler engineer

General builder

Damp-proofing engineer

V,W

Acknowledgments

All images in this book are copyright of the Reader's Digest Association Limited, with the exception of those in the following list.

The position of photographs and illustrations on each page is indicated by letters after the page number:
T = Top; **B** = Bottom; **L** = Left; **R** = Right; **C** = Centre

10 Edifice
14 **T** Houses & Interiors/David Copsey
15 **B** Houses & Interiors/David Markson
16 Houses & Interiors/Ed Buziak
49 www.CotswoldCo.com
51 **TR** GE Fabbri Limited
    CR GE Fabbri Limited
    BL GE Fabbri Limited
72 **TR** GE Fabbri Limited
    BL GE Fabbri Limited
    BR GE Fabbri Limited

73 **TR** GE Fabbri Limited
    BR GE Fabbri Limited
81 **TR** GE Fabbri Limited
    CR GE Fabbri Limited
    BR GE Fabbri Limited
82 Fired Earth
83 **T** Fired Earth
    B Elizabeth Whiting & Associates/David Giles
98 **TR** GE Fabbri Limited
    BL GE Fabbri Limited

Reader's Digest First-time Homeowner's DIY Manual is based on material in *Reader's Digest DIY Manual* and *1,001 DIY Hints and Tips*, both published by The Reader's Digest Association Limited, London

First Edition Copyright © 2006
The Reader's Digest Association Limited,
11 Westferry Circus, Canary Wharf,
London E14 4HE
www.readersdigest.co.uk

Editor Alison Candlin
Art Editor Julie Bennett
Assistant Editor Helen Spence
Editorial Consultant Mike Lawrence
Proofreader Ron Pankhurst
Indexer Marie Lorimer

Reader's Digest General Books
Editorial Director Julian Browne
Art Director Nick Clark
Managing Editor Alastair Holmes
Head of Book Development Sarah Bloxham
Picture Resource Manager Martin Smith
Pre-press Account Manager Sandra Fuller
Senior Production Controller Deborah Trott
Product Production Manager Claudette Bramble

The Reader's Digest Association Limited would like to thank the following organisations for the loan of tools, props and other materials for photographic shoots: Draper tools (www.drapertools.com)

Origination Colour Systems Limited, London
Printing and binding Everbest Printing Co. Ltd, China

The contents of this book are believed to be accurate at the time of printing. However the publisher accepts no responsibility or liability for any work carried out in the absence of professional advice.

We are committed to both the quality of our products and the service we provide to our customers. We value your comments, so please feel free to contact us on 08705 113366, or via our website at www.readersdigest.co.uk

If you have any comments about the content of our books, email us at gbeditorial@readersdigest.co.uk

ISBN-13: 978 0276 44187 5
ISBN-10: 0 276 44187 7
BOOK CODE: 400-287-01
ORACLE CODE: 250005871H.00.24